Routledge Reviva

Sin and Sex

Sin and Sex

Robert Briffault

Routledge
Taylor & Francis Group

First published in 1931 by George Allen & Unwin Ltd.

This edition first published in 2018 by Routledge
2 Park Square, Milton Park, Abingdon, Oxon, OX14 4RN
and by Routledge
52 Vanderbilt Avenue, New York, NY 10017, USA

Routledge is an imprint of the Taylor & Francis Group, an informa business

© 1931 Taylor & Francis

Publisher's Note
The publisher has gone to great lengths to ensure the quality of this reprint but
points out that some imperfections in the original copies may be apparent.

Disclaimer
The publisher has made every effort to trace copyright holders and welcomes
correspondence from those they have been unable to contact.
A Library of Congress record exists under ISBN:

ISBN 13: 978-0-367-13966-7 (hbk)
ISBN 13: 978-0-367-13971-1 (pbk)
ISBN 13: 978-0-429-02944-8 (ebk)

SIN AND SEX

SIN AND SEX

BY

ROBERT BRIFFAULT

WITH AN INTRODUCTION BY

BERTRAND RUSSELL

LONDON
GEORGE ALLEN & UNWIN LTD
MUSEUM STREET

FIRST PUBLISHED IN 1931

PRINTED IN GREAT BRITAIN BY
NORTHUMBERLAND PRESS LIMITED, NEWCASTLE UPON TYNE

INTRODUCTION

IN ethics, as in every department of human thought, there are two kinds of opinions, namely, those based upon tradition on the one hand, and on the other hand, those having something in their favour. The following pages constitute an able and vigorous attempt on the part of Mr. Briffault to induce his readers to base their ethical opinions upon something other than the prejudices of the average members of the last generation. The writer on ethics is in the awkward position that, since his opinions are concerned with right and wrong, those who differ from him consider him not merely mistaken, but wicked. This attitude makes the rational discussion of ethics very difficult. It is, however, a help to become aware, as the study of anthropology makes one aware, of the extraordinary diversity of customs which have been considered moral in different times and places. If, as our conventional moralists would have us suppose, the tradition of the elders of the tribe is the ultimate authority in ethics, we are forced to conclude that virtue is local and topical. This conclusion is intolerable to a philosophic mind, which cannot but desire to derive virtue from some general principle, such as justice, or happiness, or wisdom, or what not. An honest attempt to derive virtue from no matter what general principle is certain at many points to conflict with what is purely traditional. It will not, however, on this account be ill thought of except by those to whom a philosophic outlook is impossible.

The reader will find in Mr. Briffault's pages a great deal of matter for his earnest consideration. To a distinguished anthropologist such as Mr. Briffault, the extent to which opinions having a purely superstitious origin

5

persist in each one of us from mere force of habit has been made evident by his studies, but to most of us the influence of habit upon our ethics is difficult to realize, especially as the reaction of self-protective indignation often enables us to repel even the most powerful assaults of reason. To any reader who feels inclined to indulge in indignation at any of the contents of the following pages, I would suggest that his emotion is evidence of his unreason and of the importance of attempts to teach him to view traditional tabus calmly. If two men disagree as to whether Egypt or India was the source of civilization, this is not taken as evidence of the depravity of either, but if they disagree as to the chastity of ancient Egyptian women, this is taken to prove that one of them is a lewd fellow.

Mr. Briffault may be right or may be wrong in any particular opinion that he expresses, but in one respect, and that the most important, he is certainly profoundly right, namely, that his appeal is to reason and not to prejudice. It is curious that men and women who can think rationally upon every other subject often have their minds completely closed to argument where sex is concerned. This attitude is causing a very great deal of preventable unhappiness, and it is the duty of everyone who does not wish to promote misery to do what he or she can in the way of becoming as reasonable on this as on other subjects. In old days the territory of superstition embraced agriculture, the criminal law, journeys, funerals, indeed practically everything that was regarded as important; gradually it has become restricted until almost nothing is left within it except sex. I hope that Mr. Briffault's book will contribute, as it is well calculated to do, to the dislodging of superstition from this last remaining stronghold.

CONTENTS

I

MORAL TRADITION AND REASON

THE moral tradition of Western civilization derives from Christianity, and through Christianity from Judaism. Most other elements of that civilization, such as the forms of its philosophical and scientific thought, of political ideas, of literature and art, derive ultimately from ancient Greek culture. But morality, being regarded as part of religion, the ideas and principles of the Greeks, who devoted an enormous amount of attention to the discussion of ethics, or morals, have been set aside, and in their stead the ideas and principles of the ancient Christians and Jews have been adopted as the foundation of the moral conceptions of the Western world.

They were entirely different from those of the Greeks. The ancient Jews attached as much importance as the Greeks to the task of achieving righteousness. The constant disappointment of their political ambitions, their long humiliation as tributaries of the Assyrians, Egyptians, Babylonians, Persians, and Romans, caused them to seek refuge and consolation in the consciousness of superior righteousness. But their notion of what constitutes righteousness or morality remained much more primitive than that of the Greeks. They did not, like the latter, devote much attention to discussing the question. Their answer to it was a simple one. " It shall be our righteous-ness," they said, " if we observe to do all the command-

9

ments before the Lord our God, as he hath commanded us " (*Deut.* v. 25).

The Law of God, as set forth in the Book of the Law, which the scribe Shaphan, the son of Azaliah, brought forth, under King Josiah, from the temple of Zion, laid down various social rules for the protection of life, of property, and the rights of marriage, similar to those enjoined in the laws of other peoples of Western Asia. It also laid down numerous ritual rules, such as those for the observance of the Sabbath at the various phases of the moon, the feasts of Passover, of First-fruits, and the Festival of Booths. It likewise enjoined the observance of sundry traditional customs. The Law of God laid down, for example : " thou shalt not sow thy vineyard with divers seeds; lest the fruit of thy seed which thou hast sown, and the fruit of thy vineyard be defiled "; " thou shalt not plough with an ox and an ass together "; " thou shalt not muzzle the ox when he treadeth out the corn "; " he that is wounded on the stones, or hath his privy member cut off, shall not enter into the congregation of the Lord "; " thou shalt not bring the hire of a whore, or the price of a dog into the House of the Lord thy God."

The observance of those various commandments, all of which derived their moral authority from the Law of God, constituted for the ancient Jews righteousness or moral excellence. A breach of them constituted transgression, or sin. If any distinction was made as regards the respective degree of moral obligation attaching to those laws, it was in the direction of setting a higher importance on those having a traditional or ritual character than on those having reference to social relations. For example, in cases of theft, it was laid down that the thief " should make full restitution; if the theft be certainly found in his hand alive, whether it be ox, or ass, or sheep, he shall restore double " (*Ex.* xxii. 3, 4). With regard to the observance of the Sabbath, however, it is laid down that " every one that defileth it shall surely be put to death " (*Ex.* xxxi. 14).

The view taken by the ancient Jews of what constitutes righteousness was very similar to that which obtains among most peoples in early stages of culture. Among all savages what corresponds to moral conduct rests upon the traditional customs of the tribe, to which a sacred character is attached, and which are usually held to be commandments issued by some divine personage. A far greater importance is attached by savages to rules of conduct which have reference to magic ideas or superstitions, such as abstaining from work at the new moon, or from breaking the bones of a slain animal, or avoiding contact with a menstruating woman, than to those which enjoin abstention from the inflicting of injuries on others, such as the prohibition of murder or theft. The latter rules are usually observed by savages as a matter of course, so far, at least, as regards members of their own tribe. The punishment of any social offence is left to the injured party. Breaches of superstitious customs, or as they are called in Polynesia, tabus, are, on the other hand, regarded as a matter of the utmost gravity. They concern not individual members of the community only, but the whole tribe, for they are held to excite the wrath of supernatural beings and to bring down punishment upon the entire community.

The conceptions of the ancient Jews concerning righteousness, or morality, retained that primitive character. For they did not rest upon considered conclusions resulting from the discussion of what is socially beneficial, but upon the authority of tradition. And therefore whatever enjoyed the authority of tradition, however difficult it might be to perceive in what manner it might serve any useful purpose or be in any way meritorious, was regarded as possessing moral authority on no other ground than that of established tradition. Unlike many of their neighbours, the Jews regarded all social regulations, such as those having reference to commercial transactions or to the treatment of slaves, as part of the Law of God. In other words, they had no civil law. Other nations, such as the Babylonians, had codes of civil law promulgated by the head of the State and resting upon the authority of the government. But with the Jews all laws were understood to rest upon divine authority, and to be direct behests of their god. All therefore enjoyed equal authority as moral commandments. And that moral authority applied equally to rules of conduct which served an obvious social purpose, and to rules of conduct the purpose of which was not obvious, but which had been handed down by tradition from primitive times.

Towards the same time as the ancient Jews were setting down the rules of their moral tradition, the Greeks, in another part of Western Asia, were also occupied with the consideration of morals, or righteousness. But they approached the question from a totally different point of view. They set aside and repudiated entirely, in these matters, the authority of tradition, and applied themselves to weighing and discussing what forms of behaviour were beneficial and which were injurious. Taking the matter up from that point of view, they, of course, were wholly unconcerned with superstitious customs the object of which was not obvious, and which did not appear to result in any sort of benefit to anyone. In their endeavour to gain a clear idea of what is right and what is wrong they arrived at the conclusion that the whole of righteousness, morality, or right conduct may be summed up in one word : justice.

Thus, for example, one of the oldest of those Greek wise men, Herakleitos of Ephesos, insisted that the distinction between right and wrong has nothing whatever to do with the authority of divine commandments, for " God," he said, " is beyond good and evil. To Him all things are fair and good. The distinction between what is right and what is wrong is a human distinction. It depends upon the evil behaviour which is apt to arise among men. We should not know that there is such a thing as justice if there were not men who behave unjustly. To be just is to abstain from behaving unjustly towards other people."

Or again, another ancient Greek, whose name, Epikouros, has been branded as standing for all sorts of immorality, expressed his immoral ideas as follows : " Justice, or righteousness," he said, " is what leads men to abstain from inflicting any form of injury upon their fellows. If a rule of conduct is established in human tradition which serves no useful purpose in achieving that object, that rule has nothing to do with righteousness. If it is merely declared to be a part of morality by common tradition, and yet cannot be perceived by ordinary reason to be really just, it is nothing but a vain opinion. In like manner when social conditions change, a thing which was formerly held to be moral may no longer serve any useful purpose under the changed conditions, and it therefore ceases to be moral or just from the moment that it ceases to perform any beneficial function."

The views of the ancient Jews and those of the ancient Greeks on the subject of righteousness or morals differed, it will be seen, profoundly in principle. All honest opinions are, we are accustomed to consider, entitled to respect. But it is hard to see that the honest opinion of the ancient Jews and the honest opinion of the ancient Greeks are both entitled to the same respect. For the one is clearly reasonable and the other is not reasonable. If ancient tradition is the test of what is right or wrong, it is clear that whatever the rudest ancient savages thought right must continue to enjoy absolute moral authority in the twentieth or in the thirtieth century. Such a principle as the foundation of morals is not only unreasonable, but it is clearly apt to be outrageously objectionable. If that principle be adopted, what claims to be moral is liable to be in fact intolerably immoral. And far from being entitled to respect, that honest opinion, which assigns indisputable moral authority to whatever happens to be handed down by tradition from savage times, is an abuse which civilized men and women have the right to object to most strongly, and an injustice which they are entitled to fight tooth and nail. Honest opinions in astronomy or biology are entitled to respect; that is to say, they are entitled to be discussed and sifted with judicial frigidity, and no blame is imputable to the upholders of foolish opinions in astronomy or biology except that they are foolish. But it is a different matter with opinions by which conduct is regulated. A foolish opinion in morals is not merely foolish, it is immoral. It is immoral because it inevitably inflicts injuries and injustice on people, and whatever inflicts unjust injury is immoral. People therefore have a right to resist foolish opinions in morals, which is quite different from their right to controvert foolish opinions in astronomy or biology. They have a right to defend themselves against injury and injustice. And it is quite irrelevant to claim respect for honest opinions which inflict injustice and injury, and are therefore immoral. The principles which governed the notions of righteousness of the ancient Jews and those which governed those of the ancient Greeks are not entitled to an equal measure of respect.

Christianity added many new and important elements and principles to the moral conceptions of Judaism and discarded many others. In many respects Christian morality was a great advance on the morality of the ancient Jews as set forth in the Law of God. But it retained the fundamental principle upon which moral authority was held by the ancient Jews to be founded. It continued to regard moral obligation as resting on divine commands, and as possessing an absolute authority on that account, unquestionable and not open to discussion. Christianity, like Judaism, founds moral obligation on the authority of tradition, and not like the ancient Greeks on the authority of reasonable conclusions as to what is and what is not just and beneficial in human relations. Christianity continues at the present day to offer the same definition of what constitutes righteousness and what constitutes sin as was given in the Book brought out of the temple of Zion by scribe Shaphan. It defines sin: " any want of conformity or transgression of the Law of God " (*Shorter Catechism*).

While we derive most of the notions upon which modern Western civilization is built from the ancient Greeks, who put their trust in reason, free inquiry, and discussion, the morals, the notions of right and wrong which obtain in Western civilization, repudiate the Greeks' confidence in reason and inquiry, and set up instead the authority, unquestionable and categorical, of established tradition. It therefore assigns, like the ancient Jews, the same authority to tabus which have their origin in the superstitious ideas of savages and to rules of conduct which are dictated by the requirements of social life, by justice in social relations, and by concern for human welfare.

The reason for the utterly different attitude and standards which are adopted by Western civilization in regard to science, or politics, and in regard to morals, is that the latter are held to belong to the province of religion. It is therefore not possible to discuss the morals of Western civilization in the same manner as one might discuss astronomy, biology, or politics, for the morals of Western civilization being founded on religion, they cannot be discussed without challenging the fundamental principle upon which they rest. Astronomy, biology, and other sciences have gained the right to be discussed without reference to the dogmas of religion. Morals have not yet established that right. To do so would be to revert in morals, as has been done in science or in politics, to the point of view of the ancient Greeks, and to abolish the change which was effected by Christianity when for the principles of the ancient Greeks it substituted those of the ancient Jews.

II

MORALS AND TABUS

To seek after righteousness is one of the most estimable aims that a man can set himself, indeed by common consent the most estimable. Estimable because the well-being and the very security and life of men and women largely depend upon the manner in which other human beings behave towards them. Everyone is therefore anxious above all things that other people should strive after righteousness. Righteousness, or as the Greeks termed it, ethics, or as the Romans called it, morality or morals, is accordingly accounted supreme among human values. But the value of righteousness does not depend upon the intentions of those who seek after it, but upon the effects of their conduct. To seek after righteousness and instead of promoting the well-being of men and women, to bring them misery, is not righteous or moral. It is profoundly unrighteous and immoral. A half-dozen words set down by scribe Shaphan in the Book of the Law have caused several thousands of women in England, Scotland, and America to be cruelly put to death. The righteous intentions of scribe Shaphan and of those who were zealous for the Law of the Jewish God were therefore in this instance not estimable, but abominable, detestable, profoundly unrighteous and immoral. It is quite possible, therefore, for seekers after righteousness to be the most pestilently unrighteous people in the world, and for what is regarded by them as moral to be shockingly and outrageously immoral. The persecution

18

of persons accused of witchcraft is not by any means the only instance in which the adoption of the Law of the Jewish God by Christian Europe as the standard of righteousness and morality, instead of furthering the well-being of men and women, has had the exactly opposite effect. Innumerable forms of intense misery are caused at the present day by the standards of righteousness or morality which have been adopted in the tradition of Western civilization.

Indeed, from the moment that righteousness or morality is regarded, not as intended to promote human well-being, but as a dogmatic, categorical law, the authority of which is not to be questioned, there exists no guarantee that to seek after righteousness will not be the most pernicious purpose that can inspire the behaviour of human beings towards one another. And that is in fact the usual and inevitable effect of dogmatic morality. Absolutism in morals is a guarantee of objectionable morals in the same way as absolutism in government is a guarantee of objectionable government.

With the early Greek thinkers the pursuit of righteousness was safe because they did not regard righteousness as a categorical imperative or a divine law, but as subject, like all human thought, to the standards of reason. A categorical moral imperative means a rule about which it is irrelevant to ask any question. The wise men of Greece, before they had heard the fame of the Jewish God or seen his glory, called righteousness justice, and held that whether a form of conduct is righteous or unrighteous is a question open, like any other, to discussion, and one which may be answered by ascertaining whether that conduct promotes human well-being or not. They considered, in other words, that with reference to every principle of morality the question " Why? " should be asked and should be susceptible of a rational and intelligible answer. After the Jews had declared the glory of God among the Gentiles and the islands afar off, righteousness and morality ceased to be regarded as open to discussion, and became instead a categorical imperative. The question " Why? " was no longer held to be relevant or even permissible. Until the last few years it was indeed considered wicked and objectionable to discuss some aspects of morality. In the year 1901 an eminent man of science was, in England, prosecuted, fined, and threatened with imprisonment for discussing morality. A few days ago the Dean of St. Paul's reiterated his opinion that morality should not be discussed, and that the disposition shown by present generations to discuss morality was a sign of the degeneration and depravity of the times. The Dean of St. Paul's view is an effect of the declaration of the glory of the Jewish God among the Gentiles.

Some of the morality adopted from the Jews by Western civilization is plainly justifiable on rational grounds. For example, in the Law of God is laid down the principle: " Thou shalt not kill." If it be asked " Why? " the answer is obviously that social life would be impossible if people did not bridle their inclination to murder one another. But with reference to other principles laid down in the Law of God the answer to the question " Why? " is neither obvious nor simple. For example, it is set down in that Law as a moral principle of equal authority with the prohibition of murder : " Keep the Sabbath day to sanctify it; in it thou shalt not do any work." If, in this instance, it be asked " Why? " no answer can be given without going into the superstitious notions of savages concerning unlucky days and the tabus to be observed at the various phases of the moon. Those anthropological considerations, however interesting, have nothing to do with the purpose of righteousness or morality. It is true that, as with several other principles of European moral tradition which do not appear to be directly intended to promote human welfare, but are the outcome of superstitious ideas, certain advantages may be adduced which nevertheless accrue from the observance of the rule. Those advantages are even, in the instance of Sabbath-observance, fairly obvious. That a day should from time to time be set aside in which a truce is called in the strenuous efforts of men to obtain one another's money is highly beneficial. Were there no Sabbath, it would in any scheme of social order be a very desirable provision that such days should be appointed. But it should be clearly noted that, in this and in all similar instances, the advantages which may be mentioned as resulting from the observance of the rule are not the consideration which has led to its adoption and leads to its enforcement. And this makes all the difference. People are disposed to say : " What does it matter what the original motive for the observance may have been, so long as it has beneficial effects? " It makes, I repeat, in every such instance a world of difference. For a rule which is not imposed and enforced for a beneficial purpose, but for a quite other reason, is always a source of tyrannous abuses which inflict injury and quite outweigh any beneficial effects which may incidentally arise from the observance of the rule.

The Puritan Sabbath, not being intended to bestow upon men and women the benefit of a truce in their toils and cares, but having quite other objects in view, is observed in a manner which inflicts discomforts and injustices that are out of all proportion to the incidental benefit. In the industrial districts of England and Scotland at the present day the chief effect of Sabbath-observance is to deprive hard-working people of any opportunity for enjoyment on the only day on which such opportunity might be open to them. Sabbath-observance has been, and is still enforced by those who regard ancient Hebrew literature as the foundation of righteousness with a zeal, a ferocity, a disregard of human welfare which bear no relation to the beneficial value of a day's rest. It was not long since a misdemeanour in Scotland to walk in the streets during service hours, and in New London, Massachusetts, John and Sarah Chapman were apprehended and brought before the court in 1670 " for sitting together on the Lord's Day, under an apple tree in Goodman Chapman's Orchard." At Bury, in Suffolk, the by-laws appointed that boys found in the street on Sundays should be whipped. " If they be boyes above the age of tenne years, that shall in this point offende, their fathers and their mothers that should have better looked to them, shall be punished, and the boy offendinge, by his father or mother whipped, the constable seeinge the performance thereof." When I was a boy I was very fond of skating. One winter the first day, and as it chanced the only one, when the ice in the park was fit for skating was a Sunday. I wished to go skating, but my mother was nearly ill at the thought of my doing so, and said she could not bear the disgrace of my being seen going down the street carrying skates. I went, but I did so with an evil conscience, and when I had reached the pond I was so wretched on account of the grief I was causing my mother that I turned back. It is not long since the employers of labour in the industrial districts of England evinced a strange indifference for the safety and health of those they employed. Adequate provisions to ensure that safety are now enforced by civil regulations and government inspection, not, be it observed, by appeal to religious or moral motives. But pious employers who showed criminal indifference in the matter of human life exercised the utmost ingenuity to make it impossible for their workers to break the Sabbath by deriving from the leisure it afforded any kind of enjoyment. Their respective attitude towards the two moral obligations, regard for human life and Sabbath-observance, was exactly similar to that of the ancient Hebrews who attached comparatively little importance to the former and punished Sabbath-breaking with death.

Since nothing is an unmixed evil or an unmixed good, it is always possible to adduce indirect and incidental advantages as a plea for even the most patent evils. A great deal has been said about the benefits arising from war, from autocracy, slavery, prostitution. Plausible pleas have been adduced for the Holy Inquisition, the Star Chamber, the massacre of St. Bartholomew. Advocacy is always possible. It might even be maintained that all murders are desirable because unless they were committed, society would be in constant danger from the presence in its midst of undetected potential murderers. But such pleas savour of sophistry. The plea that a principle which does not rest upon motives of justice, but upon superstitious ideas, is nevertheless commendable in view of indirect advantages, stands upon the same plane of sophistry. But that sophistry is not the sole or the main objection to superstitious tabus, for those tabus being enforced from quite other motives than that of human well-being, their effect is invariably quite other than beneficial, whatever incidental advantages may be claimed for them. Sabbath-observance would be a beneficial institution were its true purpose that of securing rest and leisure, but as that is not the intention of enforcing the observance, instead of proving beneficial, it proves an oppressive vexation. There are countless rules which are commendable as rules of hygiene, of prudence, of expediency, but if they were enforced with the ferocity with which superstitious moral principles are enforced by boards of Evangelical and Methodist Councillors, the tyranny would far outweigh any advantages of those rules. It might be plausibly argued that most people would be the better for an occasional dose of castor oil. But if castor oil were forcibly poured down their throats, they would be justified in protesting, not against theories of hygiene, but against the practice of Fascism. Hygiene and expediency do not belong to the province of morals. There is no reason why they should not be commended on the score of hygiene or expediency; when they are enforced on quite other grounds, they become oppressive abuses. It may be demonstrated that low heels are more hygienic than high heels. But if a woman who chooses to wear high heels were to be on that account taken in charge by the police, cast into prison, and treated as a social pariah, the rule would be not only an absurd Lilliputian antic, but an abuse and a tyranny which would excite just indignation.

There is a widespread popular notion that many superstitions, however irrational their ostensible motive may appear, are founded upon some subconscious wisdom. Learned folklorists have at times pandered to the popular justification of superstition. Sir James Frazer wrote a book[1] setting forth the debt which traditional morality owes to savage superstition. Traditional morality owes a great deal to savage superstition, but that merely proves that a great deal of traditional morality is superstitious, not that savage superstition is moral. As a matter of fact the popular notion that superstitions owe their origin to vague wisdom is entirely erroneous. Nothing is more conspicuous in the behaviour and mentality of uncultured races than their utter indifference to hygiene, their reckless improvidence, their lack of foresight and prudence, and their incapacity to connect cause and effect. To anyone who has had the slightest acquaintance with savage man suggestions to the

[1] *Psyche's Task.*

effect that any of his superstitions is even remotely connected with wise and provident considerations, with far-reaching foresight, with acute observation are grotesque. Superstitions owe their origin to what in savage culture stands for religion, namely, the belief in magic. That belief rests upon the endeavour to supersede and circumvent by irrational means the order of natural causation which can only be effectually controlled by rational means. It is the reverse of wisdom, the antithesis of rationality.

In the same manner as savage humanity substitutes supernatural agencies for natural causes, magic procedures for intelligent provisions and devices, irrational means for rational ones, so the rules of conduct to which it attaches the greatest importance are founded upon categorical imperatives and not on justice or consideration for human welfare. Its point of view thus corresponds to that of the ancient Jews, and is, like the latter's, the opposite of the point of view of the ancient Greeks. As the Jews attached greater importance to the observance of the Sabbath than to abstention from murder, so all savages attach greater importance to superstitious tabus than to principles of justice. They are not by any means deficient in the latter. Indeed their behaviour towards one another is in general conspicuously more moral than that of most civilized communities. The notion of the " noble savage " is not altogether a fable. Missionaries who have gone out to impart the light of Christian morality to savages have sometimes felt scruples about expounding the moral beauty of the Sermon on the Mount to people who, in their daily lives, practised its principles far more constantly than any Christian society. Even pious Puritans in New England have been put to shame by the contrast between the conduct of the heathen Indians towards them and their own conduct towards the Indians. But that moral excellence of savages as regards their dealings with one another does not arise from reverence for the authority of moral principles. It is the effect of spontaneous sentiments which arise from the conditions of primitive communities. Those communities are virtually large families, the bonds of social solidarity are much closer and stronger than in heterogeneous civilized aggregates where individual interests are brought into sharp conflict. There is little ground for those conflicts of interests where there is little private property. Where all interests are in common, mutual assistance and goodwill are spontaneous sentiments. Common interests take the place of individual interests. To assist others, to share with them and to protect them is as natural in uncultured societies as it is natural in individualistic civilized communities to rob, cheat, outwit, and defraud. Hence, while the Sermon on the Mount appears sublime to civilized people, it appears commonplace to savages. So commonplace and spontaneous is the social morality of the savage that it does not occur to him to formulate it as moral principles.

The principles of conduct which are formulated by savages are those which are not natural, but traditional. An extravagant importance is attached by all savages to irrational, useless, and superstitious tabus which appear considerably more grotesque than the laws of Lilliput concerning high heels and low heels. The breach of a rule of social morality, such as murder, is, when it occurs, regarded as a matter of private judgment, and is generally held to have been justifiable in the circumstances. But horror fills the mind of every man at the thought of the breach of a tabu, such as eating prohibited food, breaking the bones of a slain animal, gathering firewood at the new moon, pronouncing the names of deceased persons, holding conversation with one's mother-in-law, exposing the sole of one's feet, or failing to observe the rites of mourning. A man accidentally guilty of any of those moral offences endeavours to conceal his turpitude, and shrinks from the eyes of his fellows. While social justice is a matter of natural sentiments, the observance of tabus is a supernatural behest, a moral law, a categorical imperative.

The view that morality is not a matter of rational provision for social welfare, but a categorical imperative founded on supernatural authority, is the ordinary view of the savage concerning tabu rules. The notion of the Greeks that morality has nothing to do with categorical imperatives or supernatural sanctions is the outcome of a degree of civilization, of informed intelligence, and moral culture considerably more advanced than the notions of savages. Unfortunately while European culture owes most of its civilization to the Greeks, it has derived its moral tradition from the Jews, whose ideas on the subject were not those of civilized people, but of savages. Thus it is that the Scottish-German philosopher, Immanuel Kant, found it possible to discourse intelligently concerning the metaphysics, the mathematics, and the astronomy which he derived from the culture of the Greeks, and to discourse like a savage concerning the moral law which he derived from the superstition and savagery of the Jews.

European civilization abounds in incongruities. But none is so extravagantly fantastic as its accepted estimates of moral values. When morals are mentioned, it is currently understood that no reference is intended to justice, or respect for human life, or for human rights, or for honesty, truth, humanity, mercy, or goodwill. Those objects are admitted to be estimable, desirable. But they are not, in current usage, referred to as morality. They are themes of discussion, of controversy, of politics, occasions for differences of opinion held to be legitimate and respectable. The term morals has, in the acceptation current in European civilized tradition, reference exclusively to tabus on sex. When people speak of safeguarding public morals, they are not alluding to the desirability of checking fraud, spoliation, unjust abuses, of putting down war, or poverty, or social injustice, or the hypocritical immorality which countenances and upholds iniquity and injustice. In speaking of morality they are referring to none of those things. What they have in mind is the exposure of unclothed human bodies, the denotation of physiological functions and organs by other than Latin words. The world is writhing under needless suffering, it is desperately crying for justice. But the righting of injustice, the safeguarding of life, are matters for lukewarm and leisurely speculation, for speculation which is, indeed, generally regarded as of questionable taste and doubtful repute. Meanwhile " public morals " are being safeguarded, the observance of the tabus of decency is being enforced with fierce, ferocious, and effective zeal.

Such are the standards of morality which Western culture has acquired by setting in the place of the conceptions of the ancient Greeks the superstitions of the ancient Jews.

III

PURITANISM

Zeal for morality is associated with the Puritans. That is
not to say that the Puritans are more moral than other
people, but that they are more zealous. The first people to
adopt the appellation of Puritans were Anabaptists. They
were put down on account of their scandalous licentiousness. They, however, called themselves also " the unspotted
Lambs of God." The association of zeal for morality with
Puritanism is a natural consequence of the circumstances
which gave rise to Puritanism. The religious side of the
movement was only an aspect of the social and political
issue. The development of Puritanism was associated with
the rise of the burgher classes to power. The distinction
between the aristocratic ruling classes and the burghers was,
under feudalism, much sharper than any caste distinction
at the present day. The aristocratic classes were gentlemen.
A semi-moral meaning has, since the rise of burgher power,
become elaborately attached to the term—as in Newman's
famous discourse on the virtues of a gentleman. But the
name simply means a man of gentle, that is, gentile, or
aristocratic birth. Later it came to mean a man with an
income of no less than two thousand pounds a year.
Feudalism made no distinction between people who were
not gentlemen, but commoners, or in later parlance, cads,
whether they were wealthy merchants able to buy out a
penurious baron or two or ragged villeins. All commoners
were equally despised as low, vulgar fellows, and were

looked upon as cads, that is, as scarcely belonging to the human species. When burghers first acquired wealth through trade, and the power of money was used to purchase charters and guarantees from the aristocratic ruling classes, that licentiousness was regarded as a subversion of the order of civilized society and as the advent of anarchy. Grave priests, such as Abbot Guibert of Nogent, denounced those purchased civic rights as a " defiance of law and justice, whereby slaves withdrew from the obedience which they owed to their masters." Religious revolt against an arrogant and tyrannical Church was an aspect of social revolt against an arrogant and tyrannical ruling aristocracy.

The widely current impression that the success of the Protestant religious revolt is connected with the peculiar virtues of so-called Nordic races, as opposed to the inferior righteousness of the so-called Latin races, is destitute of foundation. Religious revolt succeeded where conditions permitted of the success of social and political revolt. There was at one time a serious danger of Spain turning Protestant, but the power of the Catholic Church was too great to permit of the change. The Protestant revolt succeeded in Holland where the people succeeded in shaking off Spanish tyranny. It succeeded in some parts of Germany where the feudal rulers themselves were interested in throwing off the yoke of Roman priests. It nearly succeeded in France, but after a long, uncertain struggle was ultimately crushed down by feudalism. Protestantism flourished in England because, owing to the weakness of the throne which had no pretext for maintaining a standing army, the aristocracy had from the first played off the burghers against the crown. The English burgher classes were therefore more powerful than those of any other country. It is constantly pointed out that the Puritans, whatever their faults, have proved extraordinarily successful, and the success of the Puritans has been set down to Puritanism. But it is precisely because they were able to achieve power that burghers were able to assert their Puritanism. They have been able to enforce their religious views because they have been able to obtain political power. Their political power is not the result of their religious views, but, on the contrary, their religion is the result of their political advantage.

Puritanism was a successful burgher revolt against aristocratic rulers who poured contempt upon them. The English middle classes did not, however, fully succeed in casting off their disabilities until less than a hundred years ago, when they forced by the threat of armed revolution the Reform Bill upon the ruling classes. The zeal for superior morality of the Puritans was, like the zeal for superior morality of the ancient Jews, the refuge of humiliated self-esteem. It was the natural reaction of frustrated ambition against the contempt of arrogant aristocratic rulers.

When Christianity was first imposed upon European peoples on account of its political advantages, Christian ascetic morality remained for the most part a dead letter. The ruling classes never adopted it. Feudal aristocracies have never shown the slightest disposition to refrain from using their opportunities for enjoyment. They have, on the contrary, always been eager to indulge in as much luxury, festive amusement, and fornication as their power permitted. The burgher classes did not as a rule possess the same opportunities. But from the accounts of the life of the burgher classes during the Middle Ages it would appear that they were in general eager to use what opportunities they had of enjoying themselves. They were extremely fond of pageants, feasts, fairs, dancing, sports, dramatic shows, and were addicted in no small measure to good cheer and fornication. Mediæval documents assert that the English and the Scots were notable for their lecherous and licentious dispositions. The festivities, the dances, the May-day customs which were so violently denounced by the Puritans, were, there can be no doubt, occasions for a great deal of sexual freedom. In the Tudor age Spanish visitors were shocked at the licentiousness of English women. The English burghers' general disposition to jollity, good cheer and enjoyment has given rise to the endearing expression " Merry England."

As the conflict between the burgher classes and the ruling aristocracy grew more embittered, the contemptuous attitude of exclusive ruling classes fostered in the uncultured commoners a frame of mind similar to that produced in the ancient Jews by the loathing of their neighbours. The burghers' self-esteem was wounded, not because the contempt of the aristocracy was unjust, but because it was, in a sense, justified. The English gentlemen were one of the finest aristocracies that the world has seen. By comparison, the psalm-singing tradesman was pathetically mediocre. The culture of English gentlemen in Elizabethan, Stuart, or Georgian times was, in spite of all limitations, greatly superior to that which the pious burgher derived from the perusal of Hebrew literature or of Foxe's *Book of Martyrs*. The ranting Puritan's hostility towards science and culture is largely due to consciousness of his own ignorance. When he denounces the godless scientist, when he reviles the graceless artist or writer, and endeavours to persecute them, he is taking his revenge for his own conscious ignorance, lack of taste, and vulgarity. He knows that those on whom he is slaking his malice are his superiors. He is enraged at his own inferiority. The Puritans' galled self-esteem took, as usual, refuge in the claim to superior righteousness. The Jew Bible afforded him a perennial source of consolation. In the self-righteous vituperations of the Hebrew prophets, the complacent, humiliated Puritan found a vindictive malice so consonant with his own feelings that he needed no proof that this was indeed the Word of God. Armed with the Holy Book, the godly tinker hurled in pseudo-Hebraic jargon his denunciations against the vanities, the frivolities, the godless indulgences, the abominations, and whoredoms of the aristocrats. He took the same delight as the modern proletarian takes in inveighing against the manner of life of the " idle rich," in gloating over the " scandals of high life." The despised Puritan felt his self-esteem restored as he reviled " the followers of Belial, which say to their masters, Bring and let us drink," the fine ladies who " are haughty and walk with stretched forth necks and wanton eyes, walking and mincing as they go, and making a tinkling with their feet." No one could deprive him of the assuagement. His righteousness elevated him to heights of self-complacency from which he could admonish, warn, denounce, and, if possible, suppress. Like the Jews of old, the Puritans declared themselves to be the elect, the predestined and chosen people, the saints.

The self-righteousness of vulgar commoners only increased the contempt of the aristocratic classes. If Biblical denunciations had any effect upon the habits of the latter, it was to cause them to assert more freely than ever their immemorial claim to enjoying themselves. During the Restoration period, the eighteenth century, and the Regency, the gaiety which the Puritans denounced was accentuated. The final triumph of Puritanism was, curiously enough, brought about by the French theists (or atheists, as they were more commonly termed in England) and by the French Revolution. The revolt inspired by Voltaire, Diderot, and other infidel publicists abolished feudalism in Europe, and thus established the triumph of the burgher, and consequently of burgher morality. When, by the passing of the Reform Bill of 1832, the burgher classes of England put an end to exclusive political aristocratic privileges, the feudal ruling classes consented by a tacit pact to conform, at least outwardly, to the morality of the burgher classes, and to respect the susceptibilities of the Nonconformist conscience. Thus, through the influence of Voltaire and his fellow infidels, Christian morality was established in Europe for the first time in two thousand years among the ruling classes. The adoption of Puritanism by the English aristocratic classes in the first half of the nineteenth century constitutes what is known as Victorianism.

The superior righteousness of Puritans consists, like all superior self-righteousness, in the observance of tabus. But although Puritans look upon the literature of the ancient Jews as the foundation of righteousness, their observance of tabus extends considerably farther than those laid down in the Law of Yahu. Many Jewish tabus, such as that against eating pork or breaking the bones of an animal, have not been the object of much attention from Puritans. On the other hand, many tabus which are the object of Puritan zeal have obviously no connection with Jewish superstition. The " Blue Laws " of New England prohibited the games of shuffleboard and bowling, the performance of music on the violin or the flute. The wickedness of smoking is still a strong tenet of Puritan morality; the practice is held to be inconsistent with the gravity of religious persons, and to be equivalent to moral ruin in women. Any approach to elegance in dress was equally abominable to the Puritan. Thus Bishop Babington admonishes that : " Mans apparell is the badge of a sinner, yea of a condemned and cursed sinner, and therefore the pride of it and delight in it, no doubt very monstrous before the Lorde, and hatefull." Particular offence was given to the Puritans by modes of wearing the hair of which they disapproved. " I cannot but marvell at the beastlinesse of some ruffians (for they are no sober Christians)," says the Rev. Phillip Stubbes, " that will have their haire to growe over their faces like monsters, and savage people, nay rather like mad men than otherwise, hanging downe over their shoulders, as womens haire doth : which indeed is an ornament to them, being given them as a sign of subjection, but in man it is a shame and reproch." Puritans attach the greatest importance to abstention from gambling, from the use of dice and playing-cards, from games and " idle pastimes," from dancing, dramatic performances and all forms of festivity.

Puritan tabus have been chiefly resented on the ground that they interfere with the enjoyment of life. Many things interfere with the enjoyment of life which are nevertheless indispensable and precious. To object to anything because it interferes with the enjoyment of life is no valid argument if that thing fulfils a necessary and valuable function. But the interference of Puritan tabus with the enjoyment of life is not an accidental and adventitious drawback. It is the express purpose of Puritan morality.

Puritan zeal for the suppression of anything which may afford pleasure or entertainment is clearly related to the asceticism which is a feature of many religions, but is particularly characteristic of the Christian doctrine of renunciation. Puritan moral zeal differs, however, from the Christian asceticism which indulges in self-mortification and self-torture, in fasting, flagellation and hair-shirts. Puritan asceticism would thus appear to be more moderate than Catholic asceticism. But while the latter is regarded as a means of achieving personal holiness, and not as an obligation incumbent upon all men, Puritanism regards pleasurable indulgence as an evil in itself, and abstention from it not as a matter of voluntary discipline, but as an obligation to be enforced upon all. Puritanism does not regard ascetic self-torture as a virtue, but regards enjoyment as sin. It is therefore not concerned with practising the

former, but with suppressing the latter. It is not interested
in self-discipline, but in regulating the conduct of other
people.

The Puritan predilection for the tabu of the Sabbath
arises in part from the scope which its enforcement affords
for suppressing pleasure and entertainment. The tabu, as
is well known, is entirely un-Christian. It was as
emphatically repudiated by the Christian Church as the
Jewish rite of circumcision. The " Day of the Sun," or
Sunday, adopted from current Mithraic usage, was
substituted for the Jewish Sabbath, as a day, not of
mortification, but of festive rejoicing intended to com-
memorate the Resurrection. Puritan burgher religion was,
however, little attracted by Christianity, and much more
strongly drawn to Judaism. The New Testament doctrine
of forgiveness had a scanty significance, and the Old
Testament fury of vindictiveness a real and powerful one
for the burgher's galled sense of mediocrity. He made
the language of Jewish fury his own peculiar jargon. He
even improved on it; he called the Jew Sabbath " Sabaoth,"
thinking thereby to make it sound more Jewish,[1] and
invented the barbarism " Jehovah " as his reading of the
tetragrammaton of Yahu.

The Sabbath tabu appeals with particular force to the
fundamental Puritan desire to put down enjoyment. It
is only as a concession to frivolous human weakness that

[1] " Sabaoth," which means " armies," is given in the
first edition of Johnson's Dictionary as an alternative form
of " Sabbath." The howler gained such currency that it
was used by Bacon (*Advance of Learning,* ii. 24) and by
Spenser (*Faerie Queene,* viii. 2). It occurs in Scott's *Ivanhoe.*

all days are not kept as holy, that is, as pure from the sin of gratification. Lockhart, in his life of Scott, mentions how young Walter having once expressed his sensual delight at the rich taste of the broth served at the family table, his father immediately ordered that the appetizing decoction should be diluted with hot water. According to the standards of Puritan morality, that is wicked which affords pleasure, and it is wicked because it affords pleasure.

IV

ASCETICISM

The wickedness of pleasure which entails no injury to others is not obvious. Pleasure which is in itself perfectly innocent may be attended with a strong sense of guilt when it is known to entail necessary suffering to others. The comforts and luxuries of modern life are not intrinsically culpable or reprehensible. No moral guilt attaches to riding in an expensive car or to eating a well-cooked dinner. But when it is realized that every such luxury entails, by inexorable economic law, penury and hunger for many human beings, the thought may spoil one's enjoyment of them. The full and free enjoyment of the resources which human ingenuity and human love of beauty have placed at the disposal of modern men and women is rendered well-nigh impossible to those of them who are intelligent and have a sense of justice, of morality. Those considerations, however, do not trouble the Puritan. His sense of self-importance is, on the contrary, flattered by riding in expensive cars and eating expensive meals. The social system whereby his expensive cars and dinners entail misery and starvation to thousands is, in fact, mainly of his making, the manifestation of his burgher thrift. The wickedness of pleasure is not the outcome of reasoned considerations of justice, but is a traditional tabu which does not appertain to the sphere of discussion, but to that of moral axioms. Why pleasure should be wicked, the Puritan or the Christian has not the least notion. The question

41

cannot indeed be intelligibly answered without a consideration of the superstitious ideas of savages on the subject.

One of the most constant and general superstitious
anxieties of savages and barbarians is lest they should
excite the envy or jealousy of supernatural beings, ghosts,
goblins, or gods. They are accordingly rendered uneasy
by any unwonted stroke of good fortune, by undue
prosperity, or precarious happiness. They never omit in
those circumstances to take steps calculated to placate the
envy which their good fortune might excite in jealous
supernatural beings, as by devoting a large portion of their
perilous wealth to the gods, or by sacrificing the first-fruits
of their acquisition, or something which they value and
hold dear. For the same reason all products of Eastern
craftsmanship, such as carvings, metal-work, pottery,
jewels, bear invariably some intentional flaw. When you
are buying a Persian rug, you will immediately, if you
know anything about the matter, look for the purposive
flaw in the weaving which is the mark of its genuineness.
The most gorgeous Oriental manuscripts have a page
defaced by an intentional blot. In Eastern countries raw
meat and other perishable articles of food are never
publicly exposed for sale. The practice offers a good
illustration of the beneficial effects to which purely superstitious motives may indirectly give rise; for the care of
Oriental butchers is due to anxiety lest the meat should
be contaminated by not flies and dust, but by the envious
eyes of hungry persons. Beautiful children are in the
same manner protected by their parents from the perilous
influence of envious looks, and fond mothers are careful to

guard their cherished offspring against such dangers by keeping them ragged and unkempt. They are greatly put about by any expression of admiration bestowed upon them. This must, according to the best codes of barbaric manners, be qualified by some term of disparagement or by spitting in the face of the admired person.

On the same principle good luck is sought for any enterprise on the success of which great store is set by undergoing a severe course of self-denial and mortification. For example, in Cochin-China, among the Chams, when an important public work is undertaken, such as the building of a dam for purposes of irrigation, the headman dons the shabbiest rags, takes up his abode in a hovel built of straw, and remains there, taking only the minimum amount of coarse food, carefully keeping chaste, and abstaining from any form of entertainment until the work has been brought to a satisfactory conclusion. In India, when silkworms are being hatched, the owner of the factory sleeps on bare boards, gives up washing or attending to his person, remains separated from his wife, and eats only small quantities of the plainest food, in the preparation of which no butter or condiments may be used. His ascetic exercises continue until the silkworms have been hatched. Similar precautions are observed throughout the lower cultures when persons are about to engage in any important or perilous task, such as war, hunting, or fishing. Thus the Indians of Vancouver, when they set out on a whaling expedition, used to cut their bodies with shells and rub them with briars till they streamed with blood. They fasted for a week and were careful to remain chaste. Failure to catch a whale was commonly ascribed to some act of incontinence on the part of a member of the crew. The Baganda fishermen of Lake Victoria practise similar self-denials and mortifications. They separate from their wives, refrain from attending to personal cleanliness, and are careful to cook their food in the plainest manner. Hunters the world over adopt similar measures to avoid tempting Providence. In the island of Nias, for instance, the men who are engaged in digging pits to catch game exercise the utmost continence as regards food, drink, and sexual pleasures. They are, moreover, careful, we are told, to refrain from any unseemly gaiety during the operation, for they believe that were a man even to smile, the labour would be in vain, and the walls of the pit would fall in. They thus consider, in a true Puritan spirit, that the cultivation of a solemn countenance will conciliate the heavenly powers. Sioux warriors subjected themselves to the most severe mortifications before setting out on an expedition. They starved themselves completely for three days, they prevented themselves from falling asleep, and even refrained from sitting down or leaning for rest against a tree. They gashed themselves and rubbed their wounds with thorns; they abstained from drinking water so that they suffered tortures from thirst; they refrained from even looking at a woman.

Those self-denying ordinances of uncultured humanity, whose object is to ward off the envy and jealousy of supernatural beings, assume their most characteristic form in the rites observed when mourning for the dead. Whatever feelings of sorrow and bereavement primitive humanity

may experience in regard to the loss of its dear ones, those
sentiments are wholly overshadowed by the terror inspired
by ghosts. The ghosts of dead persons are supposed to be
in a very miserable condition. They suffer from cold,
hunger, and thirst. But their worst suffering arises from
the pangs of envy caused by the sight of their surviving
friends enjoying life and tasting the pleasures of food,
drink, and love, from which they are themselves debarred.
Even the most sweet-tempered ghost is liable, under those
trying conditions, to stop at nothing in wreaking his jealous
feelings on the survivors. An endeavour is accordingly
made in all rites of mourning not only to alleviate the
wretched condition of the ghost by supplying him with
food and drink, and sometimes with a fire at which to
warm himself and with women to keep him company, but
no effort is spared to avoid giving cause for envious feelings.
The mourners endeavour by acts of self-denial and mortification to ensure against arousing those sentiments. They
rend their clothes, go attired in the meanest weeds, smear
dust and ashes over their heads, neglect their person, gash
themselves, and are above all careful to remain chaste.
Among the Shuswap Indians of British Columbia, widows
and widowers, who are, of course, particularly in danger of
being assaulted by the ghosts of their deceased spouses,
took the precaution of sleeping on thorn bushes and of
surrounding their beds with screens of thorn.

The same measures which are adopted by hunters,
warriors, and mourners to deflect the envy of ghosts and
gods are naturally regarded as particularly applicable when
endeavouring to secure the co-operation of supernatural

beings in magic procedures, or to conciliate them in ceremonies of religious intercession. The chief Roman priestess, for instance, the Flaminica, had to prepare herself for the performance of any important ceremony by fasting for several days, refraining from personal cleanliness, letting her hair go uncombed and dishevelled and her nails untrimmed, and by abstaining from intercourse with her husband. Priests in most religions adopt similar precautions to avoid the risk of giving offence by any act of self-indulgence to the heavenly powers with whom they are about to intercede. All wizards and witches similarly exercise continence and self-mortification when preparing for the performance of magical incantations, even though they may during their actual carrying out endeavour to stimulate the energy of the supernatural powers by obscene exhibitions and lewd words.

From being regarded as protective measures against the wrath of supernatural beings, ascetic practices frequently came to be accounted positively efficacious in gaining power and influence over those beings. Thus, " according to Hindu theory," Sir M. Monier-Williams remarks, " the performance of penances was like making a deposit in the bank of heaven. By degrees an enormous credit was accumulated, which enabled the depositor to draw to the amount of his savings without fear of his draft being refused payment. The power gained in this manner by weak mortals was so enormous that gods as well as men were equally at the mercy of those all but omnipotent ascetics." In the Ramayana, the horrible demon Ravana, who is the villain of the poem, owes his power to his demoniac perseverance in self-denial and mortification. " The secret of his power lay in a long course of penance which, according to Hindu conceptions, gained for him who practised it, however evil his designs, superiority over the gods themselves." The practice of asceticism may thus be regarded in the light of a traffic in indulgences.

Such is the primitive rationale of all practices of self-denial, self-mortification, and asceticism. And when it is asked " Why is it meritorious to eschew enjoyment? " the only answer in accordance with the historical origin of the principle is that the avoidance of enjoyment serves to avert the envy of ghosts, goblins, and gods.

It is, of course, possible to suggest other grounds for the observance of the principle. The unquestionable categorical authority which all principles of primitive magic and superstition established in human tradition acquire naturally causes the original motives which gave rise to them to become forgotten. The established principle rests upon its own authority, and often comes to be looked upon as a spontaneous sentiment of human nature. If a rational explanation of it is sought, various justifications and interpretations suggest themselves. The direct and elaborate precautions which are taken by savages with the avowed object of protecting themselves against the ghosts of deceased persons come, in later stages of culture, to be regarded as manifestations of respect and of grief for the departed. The funereal blackness which falls upon a French family on the decease of their great-aunt is no longer intended to conceal her surviving relatives from the ghost of the good lady. Professors of anthropology in bourgeois universities will put forward the suggestion that the self-mortifications of Sioux warriors before a battle serve a similar purpose as the issue of a rum-ration. But those reinterpretations and apologetics have nothing to do with the authority of the principle and its general application. Fear of the Lord, humility, self-abasement, and renouncement are universal requirements of the attitude of the aspirants to the favour of jealous gods, and pride is the first of the seven deadly sins.

The avoidance of pleasure is often highly advisable. Most pleasurable things are harmful in excess. Excessive eating, excessive smoking, excessive sleep, are harmful. Excessive indulgence in artistic or intellectual gratifications, in family affection, in charitable almsgiving, may all assume a harmful character. The Greeks held very strong views on the harmfulness of excess. Like all peoples who have preserved the democratic spirit of tribal communities, they favoured a simplicity, and indeed a stern austerity, in their mode of life which we should deem inconsistent with mere comfort. Fatuous Oriental luxury they regarded as a sign of barbaric and uncultured taste. They never identified happiness with great wealth. Greek taste which delighted in the pure simplicity of the Parthenon would have accounted the temple of Jerusalem an atrocity of bad taste. The Jewish delight in tawdry display and gaudy finery is not, as we are prone to imagine, a modern trait of the vulgarity of the *nouveau riche*; it is constantly associated with the uncultured mediocrity which renders smug self-righteousness possible. It is an equally marked trait of Puritan bad taste. It constitutes that hopeless artlessness for which the English are infamous, but which is in reality the effect of Victorian bourgeois Puritanism, and which has perpetrated the Albert Memorial, the rival of the Temple of Solomon to the distinction of being the ugliest building ever erected. Greek taste was the antithesis of Hebrew and of Victorian lack of taste. The same canons which caused the Greeks to look with contempt upon barbaric ostentation caused them to view with like disgust the barbaric disposition to riot, gluttony, drunkenness, and orgy. The Romans, who were, like the Greeks, primitively democratic, though far less cultured, commented on the natural disposition of northern barbarians to get drunk and to shout stupidly whenever they were in a mood to enjoy themselves. That barbaric disposition has raised the problems for which desperate solutions have been sought in regulations of the traffic in alcoholic beverages which fill people of Latin culture with amazement and amusement. The spectacle of Anglo-Saxons of the more uncultured classes engaged in what they conceive to be festive rejoicing lends a colour of justification to such idiotic manifestations of Puritanical despotism as American Prohibition. Even the lowest classes in countries possessing the traditions of Latin culture have a sufficiently intelligent appreciation of the amenities of existence to render the mere crapulous orgies of barbaric riot unintelligible and unattractive.

The sensitive simplicity of taste of the Greeks and their democratic tradition disposed them to a disregard of sensual gratifications and of the most moderate creature-comforts which would have made their mode of life intolerable to most modern Puritans and moralists. The ordinary Athenian habitually subsisted on a few salted sprats and some olives, and what he called a banquet would scarcely have satisfied the normal daily appetite of a modern English or American sportsman. People who are disposed to sensual self-indulgence are called Epicureans. The term was also the ordinary appellation used in the Middle Ages for an atheist. It is doubtful whether many Puritans would be prepared to go to the length of abstemiousness which was the ordinary mode of life of the supposed apostle of self-indulgence and his disciples. According to Diokles, " they were content with a small cup of light wine and all the rest of their drink was water." Epikouros himself writes to a friend : " Send me some Kytherean cheese, so that should I desire to indulge in a feast I may have the means of doing so." " To accustom oneself to simple, inexpensive habits," wrote again that voluptuary, " is one of the chief means of leading a healthy, and therefore a pleasant, life; for it is not continued drinking, or revels, or the enjoyment of female company which make life pleasant, but sober contemplation."

The extreme austerity and frugality of traditional Greek and Roman tastes led to the widespread popularity in the ancient world of the Stoic philosophy, a doctrine not unlike " Christian Science," which aimed, according to Carlyle's expression, at increasing the fraction of happiness by reducing the denominator of desires rather than augmenting the numerator of fulfilment. It was in practice equivalent to the philosophy of Epicureanism which sought to extract the maximum of contentment from the ordinary circumstance of existence. When the Roman world became flooded with Oriental mystic cults and theosophies, those popular philosophies contributed to the preference shown for the ideals of a Jewish sect which professed the doctrine of renunciation.

In spite of superficial resemblances the Christian doctrine of renunciation differed, however, profoundly from the Greek doctrine of moderation. The chief objection which the more cultured Greeks and Romans raised against Christianity was that, if they sympathized with its moral principles, it was because those principles already recommended themselves to them on rational grounds. To convert them into dogmatic affirmations founded on superstition seemed to them, therefore, not only superfluous, but a degradation of their value and a diminution of their sanction and validity. Stoic and Epicurean philosophies were themselves a falling off and a corruption from the early Greek view that morality is concerned with justice in human relations, for they assumed it to be concerned with personal well-being instead. That is why a Stoic and Epicurean world was so ready to accept a doctrine which regarded morality as concerned with personal salvation. But the philosophical error founded its sanction on an appeal to reason, the religious doctrine on an appeal to superstition. The former was therefore applied rationally, and the latter fanatically and superstitiously.

If anyone chooses to lead the simple life or even a life of ascetic self-mortification, no one is entitled to interfere or object. But it is another matter when the simple liver or the ascetic hurls epithets of ethical abuse at those whose

tastes differ from his own. We may regard our friends
who like to go without breakfast as harmless eccentrics.
But our friendly feelings are in danger of becoming ruffled
when they ask us to spend the week-end with them and
expect us to fall in with their no-breakfast plan. Should
their enthusiasm go the length of moving heaven and earth
to prevent us from indulging in the sensuous practice of
having breakfast even in our own homes, our friendly
regard for their mistaken conscientiousness will be converted into hot indignation at their efforts to establish an
outrageous despotism over us. If we analyse that conversion
of a harmless eccentricity into an intolerable iniquity we
shall find that it has its root in the misconception that
personal ways of life are a matter of righteousness and
morals instead of being a matter of judgment and hygiene,
and that righteousness and morals, instead of being solely
concerned with justice in social relations, are concerned
with personal ways of life and personal salvation.

The Jewish sect whose conceptions became substituted
for those of the Greeks was one dating from very ancient
times, which went further than the general body of Jews
in its claims to superior righteousness, and called itself
Nazorim, Nazarites, or Nazarenes, that is to say, the
" protected," " consecrated ones," or saints. They observed
not only those tabus which were laid down in the Law
of Yahu for the use of all men, but also those specially
intended for the use of priests, that they might avert the
envy of supernatural powers during the performance of
magical or religious rites. That ritual purity which from
being a requirement of priestly functions came thus to be

extended to the holiness of the saintly ones, consisted in the savage practices of self-abnegation. The renunciation of all pleasures, the denying of all desires, which had hitherto served to divert the jealousy of malicious supernatural beings on occasions of special danger thus came to be accounted a virtue of universal application. During the last two centuries before the current era numerous cenobitic communities of Jewish ascetics arose in every part of the Hellenistic world. Together with theosophical doctrines connected with the notion of the Messiah and his impending coming to establish the reign of the saints, the theory grew among them that human life was, like the long humiliation of the Jews, a period of probation, and that the real opportunity for gratifying the desire to enjoy existence will only occur when the present trial-existence is at an end. In harmony with that conception it was supposed that the smaller the amount of gratification obtained in the present life, the greater will be that obtainable in the next. The Jewish theory was, in fact, like that of Hindu magicians, a system of banking. The more economy is exercised in spending our capacity for enjoyment in this world, the greater will be the accumulated treasure in heaven. Salvation from the wrath of supernatural powers is thus best secured by suppressing as completely as possible all that is pleasant and pleasurable in life. " The lyfe of a Christian man," remarks the old Puritan, John Northbrooke, " is a perpetuall studie and exercise of mortifying the fleshe untill it be utterly slaine." Christians, " instead of playing should use praying; insteade of dauncing, repenting; for joye, sorrowe; for laughing, mourning; for myrth, sadnesse; for pride, patience; for wantonnesse, wofulnesse." [1]

From the primitive savage notion that pleasurable experience is prone to excite the envy of jealous ghosts, goblins, or gods, has thus arisen the doctrine that whatever is pleasurable is therefore sinful.

[1] John Northbrooke, *A Treatise against Dicing, Dancing, Plays and Interludes, with other Idle Pastimes*, p. 179.

V

CHRISTIAN SEXOPHOBIA

AMONG the early Christians all measures calculated to secure the maximum amount of unhappiness and discomfort were accounted essential to the practice of virtue. Family affections were strongly discouraged. Wives were exhorted to leave their husbands and children their parents. All personal attachments were denounced as worldly temptations. The appreciation of beauty, of art, of literature were likewise condemned. St. Jerome who was an ardent scholar and had valued his fine library above any of his possessions, sold his books after his conversion, and gave up the study of literature as a temptation of the devil. Bodily cleanliness and the simplest care of the body were looked upon as signs of depravity. Christians vied with one another in the severity of self-denials and self-tortures. The ideal of seekers after righteousness was to take up their abode in the desert and to abstain from all human intercourse. Vegetarianism carried to the point of starvation was accounted virtuous. The more earnest Christians cultivated constipation.

Self-denial and self-mortification came, however, to be associated more and more with abstention from sexual gratification. Purity, which had originally reference to ritual requirements, acquired the meaning of chastity. The " senses " which religious aspiration aimed at mortifying were identified exclusively with sexual desire. That aspect of the principle of abnegation came to overshadow

all others, so that virtue, holiness, goodness, righteousness
became in the mind of the Christian but synonyms for
sexual continence. Thus has arisen the fantastic paradox
of European moral tradition which confines the current
connotation of the terms " morality," " morals," to tabus
on the relations of sex.

The reason for that singling out of one order of
pleasure for special condemnation and suppression is not
far to seek. It is indeed constantly dwelt upon by the
Christian Fathers. The desire for sexual gratification is
far more difficult to suppress than any other. For all their
fanatical and exorbitant ideas the Christian Fathers were
realists in psychology. They were far more realistic than
most modern writers who affect to regard sex with a
superior detachment and frigidity, and defend the old
tabus of silence by declaring that undue importance is
attached to the subject. Not so the Christian Fathers.
They dwelt upon sex with an insistence compared to
which the Freudians are reticent, and they did not hesitate
to proclaim the Freudian doctrine that in one way or
another the insidious manifestations of sex pervade human
activities. The Christian view, offensive to Puritanism
which has become accustomed to combating sex by the
weapon of silence and of pretended frigidity, agrees with
the estimate of most peoples who have not had the benefit
of that training. Orientals are incapable of imagining any
other point of view. When an Arab, a Hindu, or a
Japanese is introduced to Western literature, art, music,
poetry, to the amenities of mixed social intercourse, he
regards quite naturally and unaffectedly all those innocent

delectations of European culture as modes of libidinous stimulation and forms of pornography. When the European indignantly protests against the preposterous grossness of the suggestion, when he explains that nothing is farther from the minds of our respectable novelists, poets, painters, musicians, or of our young people or old people when they are enjoying the healthy and innocent freedom of social comradeship, the Oriental is profoundly surprised and incredulous. We call the Oriental " nasty minded," and we call the Church Fathers " nasty minded." But what is with us a matter of Freudian psycho-analysis is with Orientals and was with the semi-Oriental Christian Fathers a matter of course. And accordingly when people spoke of pleasure and of enjoying life, the simple-minded and unsophisticated Christian Fathers took it for granted that what they had in mind was fornication. The suppression of enjoyment therefore meant above all things the suppression of fornication.

That religious exaltation such as inspired the founders of Christian moral tradition is a close transformation of sexual appetites is now generally recognized. Jerome, Origen, Augustin freely avow the lechery of their natural dispositions. All other forms of self-abnegation and mortification they found no insuperable difficulty in carrying out. To sell their possessions, to tender the other cheek, to macerate their bodies, to forgo ease, comfort, cleanliness, food, warmth, sleep—all these things they could achieve with comparative ease. But the lusts of sex they could not wholly extinguish. " So long as we are borne down by this frail body, so long as we have treason within this earthly vessel," Jerome lamented, " there can be no sure victory."

The Jews never laid much stress on the meritoriousness of chastity. Like all stringently patriarchal peoples, they looked with great severity upon adultery. Being Orientals and superstitious, they feared nudity, scrupled even to see themselves naked or to be insufficiently clothed while in bed. But the desire to increase and multiply was a part of their fierce nationalistic sentiment, and so strong in their tradition was the ideal of procreation that to remain unmarried after the age of twenty was regarded by them as a mortal sin. Celibacy and virginity were to them utterly abhorrent. The monastic Jewish sects which aimed at a righteousness that should exceed the righteousness of the Pharisees departed from orthodox standards. Their zeal led them to attach to chastity, as the most obvious form of self-denial, a new importance. Their views varied; some practised celibacy, others contracted temporary marriages for the sake of increase. With none, however, did the emphasis on chastity acquire the importance which it did later among the Christians. There is scarcely a trace of it in the Gospels. The ferocious war on sex, the concentration of every moral purpose on the suppression of its manifestations, are phenomena which made their appearance only when the Christian doctrine of renunciation spread amid the luxurious cities of the Roman Empire. It became the haunting obsession of Christian thought. Continence came to be regarded not as a part of morality, but as the whole of morality. Every crime, vice, or sacrilege appeared venial beside the stain of unchastity. The Christian Fathers declared that the virtue was the supreme revelation bestowed upon the world by the Christian religion. Sex was the specific creation and instrument of Satan; woman was the agent of the devil and the ambassador of hell. There could be no righteousness and no salvation consistent with any compromise or accommodation with the powers of hell embodied in sex. Natural propagation was a snare intended to draw souls to damnation. The extinction of the human race was accounted the lesser evil.

Those delirious obsessions of early Christianity may be regarded as curiosities of cultural history, as strange phases of ancient thought, as pathological aberrations. But upon those views is founded the moral tradition of Western culture which identifies morality with sexual repression, and sin with sex.

There is a wide and persistent impression that, from whatever cause, the regard for chastity and sexual repression is rooted in human nature and has been manifested from the earliest beginnings by all races. It is generally supposed by people of culture and intelligence that, however irrational or fanatically exaggerated Western moral tradition may be in this respect, it is but the culmination of an attitude common, albeit in varying degrees, to all human culture and tradition. Those current assumptions are erroneous.

People of culture and intelligence do not in general pretend to expert knowledge in anthropology. They are but mildly interested in the manners and customs of savages; they even commonly repudiate any interest in the subject, and flippantly declare that the views of Australian blacks or Trobrianders have no bearing upon their own views and opinions. That repudiation is similar to the common repudiation of interest in metaphysics. When people declare that they neither know nor wish to know anything of metaphysics, the declaration usually means that they hold very definite and confident, though fantastically erroneous, metaphysical views. For, of course, everyone is a metaphysician, just as everyone is a composer of prose. In like manner the cultured and intelligent people who profess no knowledge of, and no interest in, anthropology are nevertheless usually anthropologists. They have quite definite views as to what is and what is not part of human nature, and having read somewhere that savages have a superstitious regard for chastity, they consider their information amply sufficient to serve as a foundation for far-reaching opinions upon the relation of that notion to human nature.

When, with the expansion of travel and exploration, numerous races that had remained in lowly phases of culture came to be discovered, and zealous missionaries hastened to set about imparting to them the light of true religion, the chief interest aroused by that new experience of uncultured humanity lay in the evidence which it might afford concerning the fundamental doctrines about human nature and human history. Missionaries were divided between the edifying value of showing to what depths of depravity human nature might sink without the guidance of the Christian religion, and that of demonstra-

ting the reality of " primitive revelation." Their first
anxiety was to prove the " argument from universal
consent," by showing that all savages have some notion
of the supernatural. This they had no difficulty in doing,
for all savages are extremely superstitious. The question
next in importance, namely, that concerning moral revelation, was more perplexing. Although the social morality
of the savages was, as we have noted, often superior to
that of the missionaries, their sexual morality was, from
the missionaries' point of view, atrocious. And from the
same point of view social morality scarcely deserves the
name : only sexual morality matters. The missionaries
were in two minds. They could not, on the one hand,
contain their indignation at the polygamy, promiscuity,
and obscenity of the savages. On the other hand, what
was to be said about the doctrine of primitive moral
revelation and the moral conscience implanted in the
nature of man? Many pious explorers laboured to set
forth how, despite many obvious lapses from moral grace,
the heathens were nevertheless conscious of their sinfulness
and manifested in various ways an appreciation of the
meritorious nature of chastity. Sometimes they described
the pure and chaste life of virtuous tribes. A body of
information on the manners of savages, to which was
also added a similar corpus of knowledge on the habits
of animals, thus became current and served to fortify
ethical conceptions. Thus, for example, the Rev. Phillip
Stubbes supplements the conclusive arguments drawn
from Holy Scripture and the Fathers by the testimony
of biological and anthropological science in the following

manner: "It is said of those that write de natura animalium, that (almost) all unreasonable beasts and flying fowles, after they have once linked and united them selves togither to any one of the same kinde, and after they have once espoused them selves the one to the other, will never after joyne them selves with any other, till the one be dissolved from the other by death. And thus they keepe the knot of matrimonie inviolable to the end. And if any one chaunce to revolte, and go togither with any other, during the life of the first mate, al the rest of the same kind assemble togither, as it were in a councel or parliament, and either kil or greevously punish the adulterer or adulteresse, whether soever it be; which lawe I would God were amongst Christians established. By all which it may appear how horrible a sinne whordome is in nature, that the very unreasonable creatures doo abhorre it. The Heathen people, who know not God, so much lothe this stinking sinne of whordome, that some burne them quick, some hang them to gibbets, some cut off their heds, some their armes, legs and hands; some put out their eyes, some burne them in the face, some cut of their noses, some one part of their bodye from another, and some with one kind of torture, and some with another; but none leaveth them unpunished: so that we are set to schoole to learn our first rudiments how to punish whordome, even by the unreasonable creatures, and by the heathen people who are ignorant of devine goodness." [1]

The worthy Phillip Stubbes wrote during the reign of

[1] Stubbes, *The Anatomie of Abuses*, i. 92.

Elizabeth. His notions of natural history and of anthropology are, however, very similar to those which modern intelligent and cultured persons gather from the most reputed authorities, and quite as imaginary. There was, it is true, towards the end of the Victorian period considerable activity among various men of science who, collating our information, shed a flood of light on the habits and ideas of uncultured humanity. But their conclusions were as objectionable as those of Kepler and Galileo on astronomy during the seventeenth century. They were not punished by imprisonment. But they were refuted by a popular school of anthropological professors who restored the notions of Phillip Stubbes on the subject and thus came to the rescue of Victorian morality. Intelligent cultured people derive their information from that authoritative school of bourgeois anthropology. Thus, to take one or two examples at random, a very able lady writer, Miss Vera Brittain, mentions in a recently published journalistic article that " the Munda Kols of Chota Nagpore, to the question put to them by the German missionary Jellinghaus (quoted by Professor Westermarck in his *History of Human Marriage*): ' May a dog sin? ' replied: ' If a dog did not sin, he could not breed.' " Or again a well-known writer on Art, Mr. Clive Bell, in endeavouring to fathom the history of human civilization, writes: " For the mass of information I have gone to that classic work, Westermarck's *Origin and Development of the Moral Ideas*. Here the suspicious reader will find warrant for every fact adduced; and here he will find a masterly account of the faith and morals of savage peoples

based on monumental learning. . . . The forest tribes of
Brazil, for instance, are inflexibly monogamous, and so
are several of the tribes of California. It seems sad **and**
rather strange that Professor Westermarck should have
to describe these as ' a humble and lowly race.' . . . I
am not quite sure what the professor means when he
says that ' among the Veddahs and Andaman Islanders
monogamy is as rigidly insisted upon as anywhere in
Europe '; but at any rate the natives of Kar Nicobar are
irreproachable. These respectable savages ' have but one
wife and look upon unchastity as a very deadly sin.' With
them as with many other savage tribes it is punished by
banishment or death. ' It is noteworthy,' says Westermarck, ' that this group of peoples ' (the group that feels
quite nicely in these matters) ' belong savages of so low
a type as the Veddahs of Ceylon, the Igorots of Luzon,
and certain Australian tribes.' " [1]

The authority to which Miss Vera Brittain and Mr.
Clive Bell refer is, as the latter states, the " classic "
source of information for persons of culture at the present
day, and is invariably referred to for information upon
those far-reaching facts. The information conveyed by that
authority is as accurate and reliable as that of the Rev.
Phillip Stubbes. Every one of the statements above
mentioned is false. Thus the irreproachable natives of
Kar Nicobar are, according to unimpeachable modern
observation, " singularly unfettered by convention " in
their sexual relations. " There seems to be no objection
to a girl having as many lovers as she likes before

[1] Clive Bell, *Civilization*, pp. 16, 23.

marriage, and altogether the state, when entered upon, is one that presses very lightly on the people." The Andaman Islanders have the recognized right to kill a girl who refuses their advances, and they have sexual connection in public. The Veddahs of Ceylon send any girl with whom they cohabit back to her people whenever they get tired of her; unattached women are recognized public property. Among the Igorots of Luzon " there is no such thing as virtue," and " they have no conception of modesty "; unmarried girls have complete freedom and solicit both boys and married men. They are particularly lascivious. Among the Australian aborigines " chastity as a virtue is absolutely unknown among all the tribes of which there are records." [1]

Ordinary thoughtful and educated persons are naturally perplexed by the glaring contradictory views of anthropologists, and wonder whether it is not possible to prove anything by a selection of anthropological reports. It is, as is clearly shown by our " classical " authorities. But it is generally quite easy to get at the actual facts by not selecting, but by the more laborious process of collating available information.

The Fathers of the Church proved themselves, as I have remarked, more realistic in facing facts than the classic authorities of modern bourgeois civilization. They expressly declared that the revelation of the intrinsic merit of chastity was due exclusively to the Christian religion, and that antecedently to that revelation all peoples had failed to

[1] For detailed references to, and discussion of, authorities, see the author's *The Mothers*, Vol. II, pp. 47 ff., 57 ff., 295 f.

perceive the moral worth of chastity, and had been lewd, sensual, and impure.

There does not exist a particle of evidence to invalidate the declaration of the Christian Fathers. The myth evolved by old Jesuit missionaries, popularized by Victorian classic authorities on anthropology, and disseminated for the information of cultured persons, is of exactly the same scientific value as the views of the Rev. Phillip Stubbes. It owes any colour of plausibility which makes its dissemination possible and its falsity more misleading to such facts as those to which reference has already been made. Chastity, as well as other forms of self-mortification, is regarded as calculated to avert the envy of ghosts and other supernatural beings. The sexual functions are regarded by uncultured humanity as mysterious, and much of primitive superstition centres round them, but they are nowhere regarded with dread or with an evil conscience. It is sometimes remarked that savages manifest in general a certain shyness in regard to sex, and more especially marriage, and books have been written on the theme. I am quite familiar from personal observation in Polynesia and Melanesia with the manifestations referred to. Savages are shy in the same manner as children are shy. Whenever a marriage is publicly celebrated, the bride, and to a much greater degree the bridegroom, are extremely shy. They are equally shy in any situation where they have to play the most prominent part and are the object of personal attention. They are shy if they have to step out of a crowd and if their names are mentioned, in the same manner as a child is shy when he is presented with a prize at the breaking-up of an infant school. The shyness of the savage on all occasions when he has had to play a formal part as an individual has as much reference to sex as the shyness of the infant schoolboy.

There are other grounds for sexual restrictions among savages besides the fear of ghosts. One, which, however, applies only to phases of social culture considerably above the lowest, is that arising from marital claims. That is a social rule and not a superstition. Another of far wider application is the rule of exogamy which corresponds to the prohibition of incest amongst ourselves. In some barbaric societies of very advanced development, in which exclusive aristocratic classes have developed, marital claims to fidelity operate retrospectively, and the chastity of girls before marriage is demanded. That claim is conspicuous by its absence in all lower phases of social culture.

The above include all the circumstances which call for the observance of sexual restrictions in savage humanity. I say " savage," using the term in its current acceptation to mean uncivilized phases of society. But the above-mentioned social and superstitious grounds for the observance of continence are the only ones known, not to savage societies merely, but to all human societies until the Christian declaration of the doctrine that chastity is intrinsically meritorious and sex intrinsically sinful. No-where, either in ancient or modern times, in savage, barbaric, or civilized societies, in the East or in the West, has that doctrine been held outside Christianity. The Church Fathers were strictly correct in their claim : the virtue was totally unknown in the world until they proclaimed it.

The Greeks were not savages. Some consider that they were the most civilized people that ever lived, not excepting Christian Europeans. But their attitude in the matter scarcely differed from that which is universal in non-Christian humanity from the lowest to the highest stages of culture. Those thoughtful and cultured persons who are perplexed by the contradictory statements of anthropologists, and cannot spare the time to check the assertions of " classic " authorities, are in a better position to know something of the conceptions held by the Greeks of classical times. Highly civilized though they were, the Greeks were yet in close touch with primitive thought. They abounded in superstitions that are found among the lowest savages; there is, indeed, not one of those superstitious savage ideas which cannot be illustrated out of the records of Greek culture. Their general attitude towards sex was not the result of sophisticated doctrines peculiar to themselves. It was not a departure from the primitive attitude of humanity, and in fact broadly corresponded to that of most other peoples, even in lower phases of culture. So that cultured persons who are informed by " classic " authorities on the attitude of primitive humanity towards sex that savages are obsessed with a superstitious regard for the meritoriousness of chastity and with a sense of sin can to some extent check that information, for no one has offered any evidence that a revolution in the attitude of humanity has taken place leading to a complete change from the primitive to the Greek type of sentiment in the matter.

The Greeks were perfectly familiar with the ritual practice of self-denial and mortification as a means of turning aside the envy and jealousy of supernatural powers. They termed such ritual practices of abstinence from food, drink, and sexual intercourse *agneia*, that is to say, " rites of mourning," and applied the term primarily to those rituals of ceremonial mourning which were commonly observed in the popular cults of dying gods. When the passion and death of Dionysos, or of Lynos, or of Melikertes were celebrated, the women assumed mourning, performed ritual lamentations, observed purity, and practised all those observances which are universally carried out by savages at a death, and intended to ward off the envy of the ghost. The Greeks called those rites *agneia*. They had thus a very clear conception of their origin and purpose. As Porphyrus explains in detail, those rituals of *agneia* belonged to what were termed " rites of aversion," that is, rites intended to ward off evil things, or, as we should put it, they were not so much acts of worship intended to propitiate and honour, as exorcisms. They were carried out, he tells us, " not in order that we may induce the presence of the gods, but that these wretched things may keep off."

Similar exorcisms, or practices of self-abnegation, were connected with all special religious worship. Abstention and purifications had to be observed before entering a temple. Thus when, in the *Lysistrate* of Aristophanes, Kinesias asks his wife, Myrrhine, to have sexual intercourse with him in the grotto of Pan, she exclaims : " But how then could I return to the Acropolis in a state of *agneia*? " To which he replies : " There's no difficulty about that, all you have to do is to wash yourself in the water-clock."

The Greeks, like all primitive peoples, and indeed like all non-Christian peoples, had no special word for " chastity." When the Church Fathers who wrote in Greek had to speak of the new Christian virtue they were obliged to adopt the term *agneia*, using it, for want of a better, in a new sense. So that when they wrote treatises, as almost all did, in laudation of chastity, they were literally speaking of " rites of mourning." Those rites of mourning included abstinence from food and drink as well as from sexual intercourse, and whenever the Greeks referred to their favourite virtue of " moderation," they invariably associated moderation in food and drink with sexual continence. In every reference in the most austere Greek thought to the desirability of restraining the sexual appetites, those appetites are expressly regarded as being of the same nature and on the same plane as appetite for food and for drink, and any merit attaching to restraint was looked upon as an aspect of the virtue of moderation, and not as a special virtue of chastity. Such a virtue was unknown to the Greeks, although nine-tenths of their philosophical thought and literature was devoted to the discussion of virtue and morality. No people, not excepting the ancient Hebrews, has devoted so much attention to righteousness, and to leading a moral life. But that sexual continence had anything to do with morality never occurred to them.

There is a passage in Plato, in the eighth book of the Laws, where in devising rules for an imaginary community, he dwells upon the superior nature of spiritual friendship, or love, both in heterosexual and homosexual relations, over physical intercourse, and goes on to suggest as an ideal rule for his imaginary State the moral condemnation of unchastity in such relations. " For he who is a lover of the body," he says, " and hungers after its beauty as if it were a ripe grape, and encourages himself to be filled with that beauty, pays relatively little honour to the spiritual beauty in the soul of his beloved. Whereas he who looks upon the desire of the body as a thing of secondary importance, but looks rather to the love of the soul, will be apt to look upon the satiety which attaches to the love of the body as in a manner belittling the love of the soul. And because he, at the same time, esteems the merit of temperance and fortitude and of becoming prudence, he may desire to live in continence with the object of his love." That " Platonic " love is set forth as a speculative fancy in the picture of an ideal society, in which sexual communism is likewise advocated. Plato goes on to suggest that if such abstention were given the authority of a moral law " even as is now in force as regards intercourse between persons related by parentage, it would produce benefits innumerable. For it would cause persons to restrain the fury and madness of love, to abstain from adultery and from the excessive use of meats and drinks, and to be more familiar and friendly with their wives." Plato's interlocutor, the Spartan Megillos, while signifying his assent to the philosopher's reasoning, remarks that it is open to one grave objection, namely, that it would be impossible to persuade anyone to conform to it, and Plato admits that it would be regarded by most people as a " foolish and

impracticable " moral law, and that healthy young men
" brim-full of seed " would set up an indignant outcry
against any such absurd restrictions. He meets the objection
in an obviously embarrassed and lame manner by pointing
out that athletes during the period of their training succeed
in observing temporary chastity, and that therefore such
abstention from intercourse with persons that are admired
might not be as impossible as at first sight appears.

I have given an account of the passage because it is, so
far as I am aware, the only one in Greek literature which,
in a restricted sense, exalts chastity as meritorious, and it
has often been quoted to suggest that the Greeks had some
notion of the virtue. It has even been suggested that the
passage may have inspired St. Paul. It will be seen that it
is quite irrelevant for the purpose of showing that there
was any appreciation of chastity as a substantial virtue in
Greek thought. Even had Plato spoken on the subject in
terms identical with those of the Church Fathers, the
vagaries of his speculative fancy would prove nothing as
regards current Greek sentiment. But by his speculation
on " Platonic " love coupled with moderation in food and
drink and with sexual communism, Plato himself does not
show the slightest inkling of the Christian notion of chastity
as *per se* meritorious.

If the Greeks who were highly civilized, profoundly
interested in moral questions, and at the same time closely
familiar with primitive superstitious ideas, regarded sex as
a natural function on the same level as eating and drinking,
and were entirely ignorant of any intrinsic merit attaching
to chastity for its own sake, we may be fairly assured that

no people in lower phases of culture has ever entertained different views, and that the whole of our literature of edifying moral anthropology which proceeds on the assumption that an innate sense of the merit of chastity is characteristic of unsophisticated humanity, and supports that theory by selected and edited citations from Jesuit and Puritan missionaries and travellers sharing their views, is of no more scientific account than so much waste paper.

The principles and the standards having reference to sex which are current in modern Western tradition and which have assumed the exclusive connotation of " morals," are neither the product of accumulated human experience nor of a general sentiment or tradition common to all humanity, but are the outcome of a special religious doctrine which arose under particular conditions in a sect of fanatics, mentally abnormal and diseased, who were in favour of castrating themselves and of abolishing procreation, and most of whom would, had they lived at the present day, have been removed to asylums for the insane. Their views were derived from savage superstitions having reference to averting the envy of ghosts and supernatural beings.

VI

SOME OBJECTIONS TO THE SUPPRESSION OF SEX

THE fact that a rule is founded on superstitious ideas does not, as I have insisted, exclude the possibility of its having beneficial effects. But it does follow as an inevitable consequence that with those beneficial effects will also be brought about harmful results arising from the fanatical enforcement of an unreasoning superstition. The objection is all-important and is of universal application to human affairs. Whenever anything which is unreasonable and unjust is defended on the ground that it is nevertheless indirectly beneficial, the defence is specious and irrelevant. The evil of unreasonableness and injustice is never made good by indirect benefits.

To take an illustration as far removed as possible from the topic under consideration. When a powerful and civilized state seizes upon a less powerful and less civilized country by force of arms, and subsequently justifies its action by pointing to the benefits conferred on that country by good administration and civilized development, the plea does not render the aggression less detestable and unjust. When an English tory defends England's flagrant breach of her pledged word to Egypt by speaking of " our moral responsibility," he is adding nauseating hypocrisy to dishonour. Only the smug effrontery of a bourgeois pew-opener, or of Lord Brentford, could be so blindly complacent as to advance the plea without expecting everyone to laugh in his face. If a friend came to me and said : " Look here, my dear fellow, you seem to be making an atrocious muddle of your affairs. You are extravagant, improvident, shiftless, and so simple-minded that everybody robs you, cheats you, and takes advantage of you. I am an experienced business man. What about my giving you the benefit of my experience and acumen, and letting me manage your affairs for you? " I should be most grateful and would give the generous proposal my earnest consideration. But if he should first knock me down, go through my pockets, and compel me at the point of a pistol to sign an authority to operate my banking account, and should then speak blandly about his moral responsibility for my affairs, I should take an entirely different view of his kind offices. It is the actual purpose and intention that count in practice, not the moral apologetics.

Should a scientist and thinker set forth the physiological advantages of chastity and the social benefits arising from sexual restrictions, there is not an intelligent person who would not listen to him with interest and an open mind. But when the defender of Puritan morality shouts : " Purity is the beginning and end of all morality. Impurity is vile, base, bestial, foul, filthy, abominable," the same open-minded modern people may venture the question " Why? "

When to that question they receive the answer : " Because impurity is damnable, beastly, unclean, slimy, odious, loathsome, and detestable," they may reiterate the question " *Why?* "

And when they are further told that all decent persons

should obviously observe the laws given to the ancient Jews by Yahu, and the principles laid down by the bishops of ancient Rome, they may still repeat the question " WHY? "

The adjectives by which the desirability of chastity is usually held to be demonstrated are terms of invective, not of logic. They do not constitute an answer to the question why chastity is a substantial virtue.

There are, of course, better answers possible, but the question is nevertheless usually answered by the ejaculation of terms of invective and not by reasonable allegations. And the reason is that such reasonable allegations as may be advanced in recommendation of chastity are manifestly feeble in comparison with the fierceness of the categorical affirmations which are usually preferred. And, in fact, those less forcible and more logical grounds of regard for chastity do not constitute the actual reason for the fierce upholding of the virtue, but are subsidiary justifications; that is to say, pretexts in the same manner as the moral responsibility of England in Egypt is a pretext, and not the true reason for pointing bayonets at the throats of the Egyptians.

When it is laid down that homicide is immoral, the answer to the question " Why? " is clear, direct, and conclusive. When it is laid down that to defile the Sabbath is immoral, or that purity is the beginning and end of morality, the answer to the question " Why? " is neither clear, nor direct, nor conclusive. That is because the former principle rests upon social requirements and the latter on superstition.

The Dean of St. Paul's, in expressing with well-cultivated restraint his aversion for the conclusions set forth in Mr. Bertrand Russell's book on *Marriage and Morals*,[1] writes as follows : " The root of the whole matter is that Christianity regards chastity as a virtue, and the breach of it as a sin to be ashamed of. St. Paul's argument does not rest on our duty to others, but on our duty to ourselves. ' What? Know ye not that our bodies are the Temple of the Holy Ghost? ' ' The temple of God is holy, which temple ye are.' ' Shall I take the members of Christ and make them members of a harlot? ' Those who say that chastity is not a virtue and that they see nothing degrading in what St. Paul mentions cannot be argued with on Christian lines. They are without that moral sense on which Christianity, like any other religion, relies. The thugs and the head-hunters of Borneo believe that homicide is a virtuous action." I single out Dean Inge for quotation because it would be difficult to find anyone who has had the disadvantage of having his mind formed at Eton, Cambridge, and Oxford and has taken up the Church of England as a profession who is more intelligent and open-minded. Yet he cannot perceive anything incongruous in placing restrictions on homicide and restrictions on un-chastity on the same moral level, and in arguing from the one to the other. It is true that, while resorting to that extra-ordinary reasoning and placing murder and the fulfilment of physiological functions in the same category, and unchaste persons such as Shakespeare or Goethe in the same class as thugs and head-hunters, he further contradicts himself, as if he felt he had not been sufficiently illogical, by stating

[1] London : George Allen & Unwin Ltd.

that the two kinds of restriction do not belong to the same category, that one kind rests upon our duty to others, and the other kind on duty to ourselves. But under the rubric of " duty to ourselves " any sentiment or superstition may obviously be declared to be a moral principle. The headhunters of Borneo believe that to procure heads of enemies is a duty they owe to themselves. The Australian black thinks that to kill a menstruating woman with whom he has come in contact is a duty to himself. The Christian thinks, as I do, that his body is the Temple of the Holy Ghost, and therefore regards his body as vile and its functions as base. The logic is again not obvious. But, as Dean Inge points out, it is not a matter of logic any more than it is a matter of our duty to others, but is purely a question of Christian tradition, and into the nature of that tradition it is irrelevant to inquire. Dean Inge is an eminent Greek scholar. If he were to take the trouble to translate his argument into Greek, he would be obliged to say : " The root of the whole matter is that Christianity regards *agneia* as a virtue. . . . Those who say that *agneia* is not a virtue cannot be argued with on Christian lines." And if he turned to his Eusebius (*Præparatio Evangelica*, IV, xxiii. 3) he would find that his argument really reads : " Those who say that the rites of mourning and aversion practised in order to ward off evil supernatural things are not a virtue cannot be argued with." Those who believe that morality consists in our duty to others do not admit that superstitions, even if called " duty to ourselves," are morality.

When saying that the grounds for the restrictions placed

upon the sexual appetites by Christianity are superstitious, I am not, be it noted, saying that there are no grounds for placing restrictions on the sexual appetites. The relations between the sexes being social relations, social requirements, that is, our duty to others, impose many restrictions upon those relations. Duty to ourselves, which is not morality, but wisdom and prudence, impose many more. The question is not whether restrictions should or should not be placed on the sexual appetites, but whether they should be imposed on rational or on superstitious grounds. And, as has been noted, when rules of conduct are founded on false grounds they are prone to have injurious effects, and when they are founded on superstitious grounds those injurious effects are prone to be intolerably injurious.

Not only are there just and reasonable grounds for restrictions on the sexual appetites, there are even plausible grounds for the Christian view that they should be suppressed altogether. The sexual appetites are, in fact, the most disturbing factor in human affairs. The French saying, " *Cherchez la femme*," is so tragically true in most of the upheavals of human life as to be scarcely humorous. The sexual appetites are disturbing in regard to all other aims of life because they are more potent and biologically fundamental than any others. They therefore operate recklessly, imprudently, and are liable to interfere with all other aims and purposes. The Greeks referred to that disturbing effect of the sexual appetites as " madness," and what they had in mind when they discountenanced sexual excesses was not so much licentious orgies as falling in love. Hence Plato advocated continence for people who are in love with one another, and the restriction of sexual activity to those people who are not in love with one another. The reasons why the operation of the sexual impulses are so disturbing a factor in human life are much more fundamental than most people imagine. Biologically the operation of those impulses is anti-social. Owing to Stubbian notions of natural history moulded on moral tradition, it is not easy to explain to those who are under the impression that animals go two-by-two, as in Noah's ark, why the relations between the sexes are anti-social. Human society is founded on the association of the sexes. That association does not exist in nature; the sexes among animals, instead of associating, usually avoid each other, and only come together for the purposes of sexual intercourse. Human society is thus a biological abnormality or monstrosity. Monogamic patriarchal societies are particularly abnormal and monstrous in a biological sense. The potent biological instinct of sexual gratification, not being adapted to sexual association, still less to monogamic and patriarchal sexual association, is thus profoundly anti-social. It cannot therefore be wondered at that it is a disturbing factor in patriarchal societies.

Such is the intractable character of that disturbing and anti-social biological factor that many intelligent people, who are neither Christians nor inclined to asceticism, have felt sympathy with the uncompromising Christian plan of suppressing sex altogether, root and branch, and stamping out the untractable disturbing factor.

There are, however, two serious objections to the plan. The first is that it is impossible. The second that it has the exactly opposite effect to that which it intends, and has made matters a thousand times worse than they were before.

Let us consider those objections.

That the forcible suppression of all unruly manifestations of the sexual impulses is impossible was, it will be remembered, the objection raised by the Lacedemonian Megillos to Plato's proposal that physical love between lovers should be put down. Plato's reply was that such complete control is not impossible, for it is, in fact, achieved by athletes training for sporting events. The objection is usually met by adducing similar instances. It is, in fact, quite true that complete control, and even extinction, of the sexual appetites is achievable, and is achieved by many persons. Whether the result of such a feat is desirable, whether the effects of that state are not worse than those of the first, are different questions. The point is that such achievements of individual asceticism are nowise to the point. The total suppression, or even the complete control, of sexual appetites which Christian morality contemplated, assuming it to be desirable, can be effective only if it is general. The exceptional feats of athletes in asceticism are no more relevant than their exceptional feats in gymnastics. They are no less exceptional after two thousand years of Christian morality than they were in the days of Plato. Nowhere during that time has the Christian plan of suppressing sex approached realization, least of all in Christian ascetic communities or in Puritan societies. The Christian societies of the first ages of Christian cenobiticism were, as Jerome himself bears

F

witness, inflamed with lust. The " Kingdom of Zion "
in New England, which offered the most perfect conditions for the enforcement of Puritan morality, swarmed
with fornication. And let it be incidentally observed that
whatever system of repressive rules, no matter how light
and lax, be established and accepted, those rules must
always be liable to infringement. Under whatever system
of morality there will always be immorality. So that it
is idle to imagine that any system of sexual morality
can ever command universal observance. In numerous
uncultured communities the only restriction to which the
sexual impulses are subject by tribal law are those which
have reference to incest, or, as it is called by anthropologists,
the rule of exogamy. That rule is not only stringently
enforced, but commands superstitious awe. Yet it is
constantly infringed. A large proportion of the instances
of alleged " regard for chastity " among savages and
of severe punishment for " unchastity " which edified
Elizabethan Puritans and which fill " classic " works for
the edification of modern cultured persons, refer purely
and simply to the prohibition and punishment of incest.
The savage virtue of the Nicobar Islanders who " look
upon unchastity as a very deadly sin," for example, which
so impressed Mr. Clive Bell, and which is extracted from
the account of an old missionary who had not the remotest
idea of the tribal organization of primitive peoples, turns
out on investigation to have no reference whatever to
" unchastity," but to incest. Christian moralists still look
forward, with incredible simplicity of mind, to some
future time when the views of ascetics will be shared

by all and universally acted upon. No opportunity, no power has been lacking to achieve that end, and no means neglected. English public schools, for instance, are conducted by priests, and one of their chief objects is to inculcate Christian morality. English public schools, nevertheless, do not turn out ascetics. To stamp out life from the face of the earth would be a comparatively easy task. To stamp out the primal biological force which actuates life is not possible.

It might be reasonably supposed that even though the ideal plan of repressing the sexual appetites by every contrivable means might, like all human ideals, fall short of complete realization, the attempt must yet tend to bring about at least some approximation to that achievement. Even a moderate amount of success would, it may from the Christian point of view be argued, be all to the good. But, in point of fact, the Christian plan has not only failed to achieve its purpose, it has in a very marked manner achieved the very opposite. The Patristic and Puritan Christian plan for eliminating from life the disturbing factor of sex has had the effect of greatly increasing the evil which it was intended to abolish. That blundering failure arises, like all failures, from ignorance. The Church Fathers were, as has been noted, a good deal more realistic in their psychology than many modern pretenders to psychological insight. But their psychological knowledge did not go so far as to enable them to realize the hard and fast psychological law that organic impulses are, like water, incompressible, and that whenever pressure is exercised upon them, their power becomes thereby concentrated and increased, and they inevitably spurt forth in another direction. That is true of all repressive action, wherever applied, but it is particularly true of so primal and prepotent a biological force as that of sex. The American Puritan plan of putting down drunkenness by prohibition laws has had the effect of considerably increasing the evil. But it is easier to suppress alcohol than to suppress a primary biological impulse. Alcohol is a product of human manufacture; the sexual impulse is, in Christian parlance, a product of God's manufacture. And, in Hosea Biglow's phrasing, " you've gut to git up airly ef you want to take in God."

The disturbing, anti-social effects of the sexual impulse which, I have been assuming, may lend some colour of justification to the Christian desire to suppress it, are immeasurably more conspicuous in Christian civilization than in the pagan civilization which it supplanted, or in any other phase of human culture. The sexual dispositions of modern civilized man are very much more fierce, haunting and protean in their manifestations than those of savage man. There has been, as in every aspect of our apologetic anthropology, a good deal of misunderstanding and misrepresentation on the subject. It has been said that primitive races are less highly sexed than civilized races. That does not appear to be true. With most savages sex is avowedly the dominant interest in life. It is for that very reason that chastity is, with them as with us, the typical form of self-abnegation. Most of the religious ideas of savages centre round sex. The power of sexual gratification is regarded by them as the one supreme value of life, and half their superstitions are intended to promote it. In the language of our moral tradition the majority of savages are extremely lewd and sensual. But in spite of their undisguised sensuality, the operation of the sexual impulses is profoundly different in the savage and in the civilized man. Necessarily so. Sexual gratification is with the savage practically unrestricted. It is therefore as trivialized as the gratification of appetite for food. That notwithstanding this trivialization the interest still remains the central interest of life shows that the savage is far from being less highly sexed than civilized man. But for the same reasons there is all the difference between the sexual appetites of the savage and those of civilized man that there is between the voracious appetite of a healthy and well-fed farm-labourer and the pangs of hunger of a starving man.

There is clearly no comparison between the sexual stimuli operating on the savage who is surrounded by nude women, most of whom are accessible to him, and those operating on the civilized man who, in the midst of the excitations of art and luxury, moves amongst women adorned with every device of opulent ingenuity for the express purpose of increasing their sexual attractiveness, not one of whom perhaps is sexually accessible to him. The virtuous and respectable savage in the Nicobar Islands, if he sees a young woman he desires, goes up to her and demands to have sexual intercourse with her there and then; and if she should demur is so incensed at her lack of common civility that he takes up his cudgel and kills her, and is held by public opinion to be quite justified. The uncomfortable civilized man who, amid a galaxy of women wearing two-hundred-guinea toilets and just out of the beauty-parlour, sees one who more than any other attracts him, merely falls in love. The sequel of the romance, should it have any sequel, will, according to circumstances, be a turmoil of illicit relations or the tragedy of, maybe, a quite inappropriate marriage. Can it be wondered that the operation of the biological sex-impulses is different in the two cases?

But it is not merely the stimulus of civilized luxury and the restrictions of ordinary civilized social life which make the difference. It is a psychological law as inflexible as that concerning the effects of repression that the earliest impressions and reactions determine all subsequent development. That law is true of all forms of development, organic, physiological, intellectual, emotional. But it is most conspicuously true of sexual activities. The contrast between the conditions of development of those activities under the loose and lax plan of uncultured morals and the plan of cultured morality is even greater than that between the kraal of the savage and the drawing-room of civilized humanity. Under the former plan, in Samoa for instance—but all savage manners are so much alike that one description applies essentially to all—children of both sexes are accustomed long before the age of puberty to toy with one another in sexual play and to imitate the sexual act. They are encouraged in those habits by their elders, and that infantile play develops as soon as they reach sexual maturity into complete sexual experience.

Abominable, revolting! But the result of those abominable and revolting morals is that there is no such thing as a crisis of puberty in Samoa, and incidentally that the relations between the sexes are rather remarkable for their quietness and moderation, the disturbing influence of sex, which serves as an excuse for Christian morality, being in Samoa scarcely disturbing at all.

Under the plan of Christian morality intended to minimize the disturbing influence of sex, a boy on arriving at the age of puberty has been thoroughly prepared to appreciate to the utmost the stimulus of diffused sexual influences. A beginning has been made in the development of his taste for art and literature. He is accordingly a far more sensitive and emotional being at puberty than a Samoan boy of the same age. His sexual instruction has been provided by his companions who are collectors of documents on the subject, which in their Christian scheme of moral education is labelled " smut." In exceptionally modern and advanced cases that instruction may be supplemented by serious personal talks by one of his teachers. In those serious talks he is told that sexual activity must be confined to lawful marriage, that he must contrive to restrain his sexual impulses until it is time for him to enter the holy estate of matrimony, and that he must meanwhile qualify for it by leading a pure and healthy life. If he be an intelligent boy, he knows that he will have to qualify for the holy estate of matrimony in quite other ways besides leading a pure and healthy life, and that he will have to spend many years of hard work before he is qualified even to contemplate entering the holy estate. His natural instincts are the same as those of the Samoan boy's, but they are very much more powerfully stimulated. He is required, he a mere boy, to perform feats of asceticism which St. Jerome, dwelling in the desert of Thebaid, starving himself, wearing hair-shirts and spending his time in orisons, confessed that he was unable to perform; which Origen, another founder of Christian morality, avowed he was unable to perform without, as he did, castrating himself. Yet, in the name of Christian morality, every boy at the age of puberty is required and expected to exhibit a fortitude which the founders of that same Christian morality declared themselves unable to achieve. The feat is, of course, in the vast majority of cases not performed. The boy masturbates. This, in his desperate case, is probably physiologically beneficial. Psychologically it is, however, disastrous. His disastrous psychological condition continues for years. During those years the victim has probably never set eyes on a woman's body. His distracted imagination is obsessed with the mystery. In current terms of Christian morality that mystery is, for the Samoan boy, shamefully profaned. For the Christian boy, the mystery is preserved holy and pure. In the following manner : his first sexual experiences are probably with some servant-girl or prostitute. Revulsion, disgust, the shattering of every youthful ideal of the joy and beauty of life, constitute in his case the preserving of the mystery holy and pure.

The ruin may not in every instance be grossly apparent. I have no desire to lay on the horror with a heavy brush. In many instances a boy may muddle through with only

partial damage. He may even succeed in the ascetic task
where Jerome and Augustin failed. It is incidentally to
be noted that the youth who does succeed in a moderate
degree is as a rule such that the gain to the race is
negligible. It is the intelligent boy who suffers.

It is scarcely possible to estimate the enormity of the
damage wrought not to the individual life alone, but to
the race, to civilization, to human destinies. The approach
to sexual life at puberty under coercive Christian morality
is not merely an evil incidental to the period of life, a
disease, like measles, which has to be got over. One of
the current affectations of hypocritical moralistic frigidity
is to pretend to regard all the more prurient aspects of sex
as immature manifestations of " adolescence." In a sense
they are. So that the entire apparatus of public moral
restrictions, the "safeguarding of public morals," is
directed against manifestations of adolescence. Those
manifestations, the carefully nurtured fruit of the nursing
of adolescent sexual life under the plan of Christian
morality for the suppression of sex, constitute the enhanced
sexual excitability which marks Christian culture. The
system of Christian morality has poisoned life at its source,
so that the whole Western outlook on sex is distorted,
deformed, and diseased.

St. Ambrose declared that, had it brought no other
blessing into the world, the Christian religion merited to
be recognized as divine on account of its having revealed
the virtue of chastity. It might with more justice be said
that had the Christian religion brought into the world this
one curse alone, the poisoning of the sexual life at puberty,

it merits, on that account alone, the detestation of the world it has infected.

The disturbing influence of sex, which has caused some to sympathize with the Christian plan of rooting out that influence, is itself largely due not to the natural anti-social operation of the sexual urges, but to the effects of the very plan for remedying it.

VII

THE SAFEGUARDING OF MORALITY

PRINCIPLES of conduct which rest on superstition always go
a great deal farther than is required by any rational justification advanced in support of them. The reason is, of
course, that the rational justification is an afterthought and
the superstition the true purpose of the principle. When
asked what is the purpose of traditional sexual morality,
most people nowadays, instead of saying that the condemnation of unchastity depends upon the fact that our bodies are
the Temple of the Holy Ghost, would say that its purpose
is to safeguard the sanctity of monogamic marriage. Far
from that being its original purpose, however, the founders
of Christian morality (who, be it remembered, were not
the authors of the Gospels, or even, as is often supposed,
Paul of Tarsus) repudiated marriage, or at best barely
tolerated it. Consequently traditional Christian sex-morality
goes a great deal farther in its restrictions than is required
for the purpose of safeguarding the sanctity of monogamic
marriage.

The tabus of sex-morality, as at present established in
Western tradition, fall into two distinct classes. There are
restrictions on actual sexual conduct, the prohibition of
adultery, of fornication. There are, on the other hand, a
host of restrictions and prohibitions which have no direct
reference to actual sexual conduct, but are said to refer to
the maintenance of decency and purity. Obviously the
scope of the two classes of restrictions differs widely. To

place restrictions upon sexual relations is a matter of social organization and of the established form of the institution of marriage. To place restrictions on apparel, literature, art, the drama is an entirely different matter. Those restrictions have no bearing on the institution of marriage or on sexual conduct, except in so far as they may be alleged to operate as prophylactic measures to safeguard the institution.

Whether they fulfil that prophylactic function is highly questionable; it is quite likely that they have the opposite effect. But in either case it is disputable whether that problematic prophylactic function is a sufficient ground to justify the equity and reasonableness of their rigid enforcement.

Here again the reason for those doubts and incongruities is that those restrictions are not really intended to safeguard the sanctity of marriage, but are of purely superstitious origin. And, in fact, when the reason for those restrictions is asked, the usual reply is not that they serve to safeguard the institution of marriage, but that neglect of their observance would be revolting, abominable, disgusting. When terms of invective are adduced as justifications of a restrictive moral principle that is usually a certain indication that the restriction is a tabu resting on superstitious grounds.

A further strange incongruity is to be noted. While restrictions on sexual conduct are not rigidly enforced, restrictions on literature, art, and apparel are enforced rigorously and with ferocious zeal. If I commit adultery or fornication, no one except my wife or the husband of the lady with whom I fornicate has the right to charge me with the offence at law. If, on the other hand, I describe my experiences in Anglo-Saxon terms, I shall at once have the police after me, and may be fined or imprisoned. The whole population of England might give itself up to unrestrained Saturnalia and set aside the sanctity of monogamic marriage, and the machinery of law and authority would be powerless to move an inch in the matter. But if a naturalistic representation of the human body be publicly exhibited, the whole of that machinery will at once be set in motion, and the Home Secretary will probably deliver himself of a grave and eloquent oration on the demands of his duty as the guardian of public morals. As is invariably the case, formal superstitious tabus take precedence in moral importance over questions of conduct.

It was until lately generally supposed, and is no doubt still widely believed, that the offensive character of what is termed indecency rests upon some form of intuition or natural sentiment or instinct. All tabus which it is difficult to justify rationally are referred to intuitions and natural instincts. That is the guiding principle of modern anthropology. After much exhaustive investigation and discussion, it is now, however, definitely known to the majority of competent anthropologists and psychologists that there is not a particle of truth in the supposition. The tabus on things relating to sex are of exactly the same order as other superstitious savage tabus. And the original intention of those tabus, far from having reference to the sanctity of marriage, or a regard for chastity, or purity, is, on the contrary, to safeguard the means of sexual gratification.

A form of the safeguarding of public morals which has

attracted of late a good deal of attention is the right claimed by established authorities to suppress literature in the interests of public morals. The right to freedom of expression in literature is one of the most important foundations of modern culture, and any interference with that right is one of the gravest offences of which despotism can be guilty. Any qualification or limitation of that liberty strikes at the foundation of all that is valuable in modern democratic civilization, and is therefore one of the most immoral abuses that can be charged against reactionary tyranny. I should personally feel as much indignation were that immoral tyranny directed against a controversial opponent whose views I regard as pernicious and immoral as if it were applied to suppressing views of my own. That freedom of literary expression is, after a prolonged and bitter battle to win it, now generally respected as regards opinions. But the principle which is tacitly allowed to apply to political and religious views is suspended in regard to the tabus on sexual decency. In England the old laws applying to that censorship leave the interpretation of their purport to the discretion of policemen and police magistrates. That interpretation is accordingly very variable. Innumerable books whose express purpose is to provide vicarious imaginative sexual delectation are secure against censorship. One test, however, is in practice definite. The machinery of legal persecution is automatically brought into operation by the use of Anglo-Saxon words denoting the sexual organs and the sexual act. The vulva, penis, and coitus may be referred to by those terms, but the use of Anglo-Saxon equivalents constitutes a final test for the suppression of literature of whatsoever kind. Those Anglo-Saxon equivalents are good English words, some of which have even a Sanskrit or Aryan linguistic status. The permitted substitutes are not English and are poor Latin. The paramount moral difference between the use of good English and that of bad Latin is not obvious.

But it becomes at once obvious when the true rationale of the tabu is understood. Among savages a large number of words are either permanently tabu or liable to become so temporarily. The names of recently deceased persons, of dangerous animals, of diseases, are with most savages tabu. The reason is, of course, a desire not to attract ghosts, dangerous animals, and diseases. The names of ruling monarchs, of gods, and of things sacred and highly valued are likewise often tabu. Among the ancient Jews many such tabus were observed. The name of the Jewish god, for example, was strictly tabu. It was represented by the "tetragrammaton," Jod, He, Vau, He, which it was, however, a sin punishable with death to pronounce. Like other things which are regarded as sacred or are highly valued, words referring to sex are often tabu. Among most savages, as likewise among Orientals, it is highly offensive to refer to a man's wife. A Chinese lady would be grossly insulted if one were to allude to her wedding-ring. Many savage tribes, in East Africa for instance, observe the same tabus as Europeans in regard to words denoting the sexual organs. If those savages possessed a written literature it would, we may be quite sure, be in no danger of being suppressed by our censors, although we may be equally sure that it would be extremely lascivious. The rule which regulates the application of literary censorship in England is thus in complete harmony with savage superstition. That does not prove that it is not immoral.

The same apologetic arguments are applied to linguistic tabus as to all others, namely, by substituting for the real motive a false one derived from it. It is commonly urged by persons who lay claim to being broadminded that, although the use of tabu words may not be breaches of the peace so serious as to call for the mobilization of the police, it is a breach of good taste. The argument is that of the lady in *Punch*, who, when her little boy inquired whether it was wicked to say " damn," replied : " My dear, it's worse than wicked, it's vulgar." The reason why it is vulgar to say " damn " is, of course, that in ages of faith it was accounted theologically wicked to do so. Victorian horror at the word " bloody " had its origin in Catholic theology. The stigma of vulgarity is only a reassertion of the stigma of indecency. A thing is vulgar because it is indecent; it is not indecent because it is vulgar. It is notorious that what was perfectly good taste in the time of Chaucer or Shakespeare is not considered good taste at the present day. The superiority of our literary taste is commonly accounted for by the mere progress of the times. But the true reason why the artistic standards of Shakespeare or Milton, or those of Swift and Sterne, compare unfavourably with those of to-day is that the Puritan middle class has meanwhile come to power and its refined taste has become substituted for the coarse standards of the aristocracy of the Renaissance and the Georgian age. Hence the superiority of present-day drama over that of Shakespeare.

Current usage, however unreasonable its standards, is nevertheless an element of literary taste. No writer is likely to adopt the habit of pointing the emphasis of his affirmations by the use of " bloody " expletives. Should his literary judgment prompt him, on occasion, to do so there is no apprehensible reason why he should not bloody well do so. Should he represent a bargee as declaring that he is fearfully sick of his job, his literary judgment would be open to criticism. So would it be if he represented him as referring to his having had coitus with a prostitute.

That is, however, by the way. The Home Secretary and the police are not paid to safeguard the standards of literary judgment, but to safeguard life and property. And whatever extended interpretation may be put upon their functions, it has yet to be shown that they confer any sort of benefit on any taxpayer, except the author concerned, by suppressing Anglo-Saxon literature.

It is equally unproven that any form of indecency inflicts an injury commensurate with the ferocity displayed in its suppression. The cultural history of the human race does not afford one tittle of evidence showing that decency or indecency has in any age of the world borne a causal relation to either the observance of the sanctity of marriage or to sexual activity in general, assuming the supreme desirability of those objects. Nudity appears to be among savage races, as in the Garden of Eden, inversely proportional to sexual exuberance. The myth that bodily pudicity is an intuitive sentiment, which was once as undisputed as the historicity of the famous garden, enjoys to-day about

G

the same scientific authority. Quite as much scientific zeal
has been employed to uphold the myth of " sentiments
implanted by nature in the human mind " as theological
zeal to uphold Adam and Eve. It is obviously impossible
to enter here into those tedious and pedantic disputes. I
have elsewhere so far sacrificed my distaste for pedantry as
to consider the question in some detail. The tabus of bodily
pudicity, far from arising out of a sense of shame in
regard to sexual functions, owe their origin on the contrary
to the extreme value set by primitive humanity on their
fulfilment. The custom of concealing the sexual organs,
male or female, is found to be preceded at all lower levels
of culture by endeavours to protect them from injurious
magic influences, more especially from the evil eye, by
means of charms and amulets which do not conceal them.
Those superstitious customs which have given rise to the
decency which our policemen take it upon themselves to
enforce for the safeguarding of public morals are originally
adopted for the purpose of safeguarding the flourishing of
fornication. The measures adopted by the savage which the
missionary interprets as indications of the rudiments of
modesty and a natural sense of sin are, in fact, exactly
equivalent to the civilized man's resort to aphrodisiacs.
Addiction to the consumption of damara is not regarded as
a virtue which it is important to safeguard. The sentiments
of which the Home Secretary and the police are the
constituted guardians do not properly belong to their
province, but to that of the rubber-shops.

The complete inversion of the motives of modesty may
be instanced by reference to their application to the female

breasts. Throughout the lower cultures and many of the most advanced, the breasts have been habitually exposed and even ostentatiously displayed. But there are occasions when even in the nudest savage women that coquetry is qualified, namely, in nursing mothers. Under those conditions the utmost fear is manifested by savage women lest occult dangers arising from the evil eye should affect the physiological functions of the breasts, and the most scrupulous modesty is apparently manifested. Western moral tradition reverses the tabu. The maternal function of the breast, excluding as it does its sexual value, is held to some extent to excuse a relaxation of the tabu on its exposure. It was not long since usual throughout the continent of Europe for women of the better classes to expose the breast in public without scruple when suckling, that being the only occasion when a savage woman thinks it important to conceal it.

Superstitious tabus immemorially established may, it is plausible to suppose, create new sentiments. The tabus of decency have not, strangely enough, created spontaneous sentiments of modesty. But they have created greatly enhanced sexual stimuli. The enormous difference which exists between the sexuality of the savage and that of civilized man is, in fact, largely due to the greatly enhanced stimuli to which the latter is subjected. That is the net effect of the tabus of modesty. The sexual impulses of savage man depend almost exclusively upon his own psycho-physiological condition. If he is sexually inactive the presence of all the naked women about him will not act as a sexual stimulus. Between the civilized man and the possession of a woman there lies a whole series of tabus, that is, of artificial sexual stimuli. And even when those stimuli do not operate upon him directly, they inevitably do so in every physiological state of sexual activity. He is consequently immeasurably more libidinous than is the savage, and anthropologists modestly put forward their discovery that savage man is of low sexuality.

"Decency" is what is beseeming or customary, *quid decet*. It is as indecent to appear in a drawing-room without a coat as to appear on the seashore without trunks, and the sense of modesty of the insufficiently clad person suffers as great a lesion in the one case as in the other. In the same manner as wounded modesty is the result of the breach of a tabu, and not of exposure, so likewise the enhanced sexual stimulus provided by indecency depends upon what is customary and not upon what is in itself sexually stimulating. Reduced skirts, when the fashion became general, were less stimulating than trailing skirts if held up above the calf. In Roman Catholic countries indecency and pornography have, from the days of Boccaccio to those of Casanova, been particularly interested in nuns. Nuns are as a rule no more attractive than other women, and usually far less. The monastic garb is expressly designed to eliminate sexual attraction. But every libertine in Roman Catholic countries is obsessed with the attraction of nuns. That attractiveness is the result of the tabu laid on nuns. The sexual stimulating value of every indecency or obscenity is in like manner provided by the tabus of decency, and the careful safeguarding of decency furnishes civilized man with enhanced sexual stimuli which are quite unknown to the savage. Those are the results achieved by the traditions of civilized decency.

Public indecency, or the suggestion of indecency, is, as every newspaper editor, novelist, or impresario knows, the most powerful of attractions. When not long ago an enterprising draper advertised silk stockings by means of a short-skirted young woman sitting in his window, the press in front of the window was so great that the traffic was blocked, fainting women had to be removed in ambulances, and the plate glass of the window was broken. It is, however, absurd to suppose, as is done, that the power of attraction of indecency, or pseudo-indecency, is due solely to desire for sexual stimulation. The public interest in indecency is only to a very small extent sexual. The commercial value of indecency depends for the most part on the sensationalism of any departure from the normal of current usage. The same sensational effect can be obtained by other departures from the normal of life, such as an accident or a murder. A " daring " play will attract so long as the " daring " is in advance of current usage. Bedroom and undressing scenes were a year or two ago worth a fortune to playwrights and managers. They have now become almost impermissible, not through the activity of the censorship, but through the acumen of assessors of commercial values. It is the unusual and the incongruous which constitute that commercial value, not sexual stimulation. Quite as good a draw as any to which the Bishop of London objects could be provided by inducing him to sing a comic song in a music-hall revue. The pretence that any censored matter, whether on the stage, in art, or in literature, is dangerously stimulating is a pure fiction. The bulk of the public on which the commercial success of indecency depends notoriously consists of women. Can it be reasonably supposed that the sight of *négligés* and silk-clad legs disturbs the sexual emotions of women? What they are interested in is not indecency, which means nothing to them, but the thrill of the unusual, of the scandalous. They are curious to know what all the bother is about, and when they have satisfied their curiosity exclaim: " Is that all? " The manufacture of scandalousness is the work of the guardians of public morals. It is hard to imagine whose morals they guard.

Their professed purpose is the protection of women and children from enhanced sexual stimuli. The profession as regards women dates, according to Plutarch, from the early days of Rome. The Romans, like the Greeks, had no notion of the intrinsic merit of purity, but we are told that they observed restraint as regards indecencies in the presence of matrons lest uxorial fidelity should be endangered. The same argument has been current in the Victorian age, when it was one of the chief duties of a woman to be shocked. The reason most commonly adduced by elderly survivors of the Victorian age for the observance of the proprieties is lest the purity of womanhood should be offended. It is scarcely needful to-day to dwell upon the myth of the Victorian convention. The modern woman who dispenses with the Victorian duty of being shocked is not necessarily more lascivious than was her grandmother, but she is, as her grandmother was and as are all natural women, realistic and matter-of-fact. The deplored decay of the

Victorian convention has revealed the fact, inconceivable to the patriarchal imagination, that a woman can be more chaste and sexually wholesome than that distorted imagination could conceive, and be at the same time entirely unshockable.

As regards the young, it scarcely becomes those guardians of morals whose policy has had the effect of converting the emotional life of the young into a sewer, to say much about their concern. The remedy for the disastrous effects of that policy is not to be sought in enforcing it more stringently. The less censorship the better in that respect. But more is required to clean the sewer than ventilation. In a rational world purged of pernicious Puritan dementia the answer, for example, to the terrifying question " Where do children come from? " would be, not a lecture on botany, but a visit to a maternity hospital. Not children only, but a large proportion of grown men and women do not know where children come from and how they come. A little personal experience on the subject would have a more sobering and wholesome influence upon their views of sex than all the treatises of the Church Fathers on the virtue of chastity. Police censorship has little effect on " the young." The chief effect of its abolition, so far as they are concerned, would be that instead of deriving their views on sex from Villiers Street, they would have an opportunity of deriving them from writers more seriously concerned with the reality of its problems. " The young " would be saved trips to Villiers Street. They would be saved considerably more.

The whole of the fictions which censorship assumes is a tissue of unrealities. Whom does indecency hurt? Did the indecency of the Bible hurt the Jews? Did the indecencies of Shakespeare or of Milton hurt their contemporaries? Does anyone really suppose that a moral lesion has been inflicted upon a single man, woman, or child by the writings of Joyce, Lawrence, or D'Annunzio? Have the tabus of Victorian Puritanism and of Christianity been equally innocuous?

One of the most curious effects of our tradition of coercive decency is that quite intelligent people who protest against the idiotic futility and vexatiousness of Comstockery and Jixity are sorely perplexed by the question where to draw the line. They assume that a line should be drawn in getting rid of an unqualified idiocy and evil. As if pacifists should ponder where the line should be drawn in the abolition of the idiocy and evil of war, and should assume the necessity of providing some scope for a little beneficial murder and devastation. The real perplexity of the drawers of lines appears to arise not from the simple fact that indecency cannot be suppressed without at the same time suppressing decency, but from dread of the immediate effects of abolishing tabus. The immediate effects of dispensing with any established folly and abuse are unpleasant. The abolition of absolutist tyranny and of feudalism in France and in Russia have had unpleasant immediate effects. The abolition of Roman Catholicism in England had unpleasant immediate effects. The unpleasantness attending any revolution, which is the chief safeguard of established absurdities and abuses, is the penalty which has to be paid for having tolerated them.

The apprehension of those immediate effects is grossly

exaggerated. It is apprehended that the entire abolition of censorships would result in an immediate crop of pornography. Possibly. But pornography can only thrive while it is considerately supplied with tabus. The abolition of tabus would be fatal to it, and the ventilation of sex with common-sense still more. The demise of Jixity would cause a slump in Villiers Street. I am old enough to remember the time when young Englishmen took special trips to Paris for the purpose of seeing the " cancan " danced. The attraction of the performance was a glimpse of two inches of bare thigh between gartered stockings and frilled pantaloons. The sexual stimulation afforded by those two inches of nudity has no parallel anywhere in the world at the present day. The young Englishman of to-day goes to Paris, though not quite so generally, to behold complete nudity on the music-hall stage. He is encouraged to do so by the Puritan declaration that the stage is converted into a brothel. After the first momentary shock of novelty, the extremely artistic use made of very beautiful English nudity at the *Folies Bergères* has in general the effect of a very sanitary flushing out of his whole sexual outlook. The admission of nudity on the French stage is one of the most beneficial moral reforms which has taken place in our time. It has done more good for public morals than all the sermons that have ever been preached.

There is not the slightest reason why we should discard clothes in the interest of public morals. It would be extremely inconvenient and uncomfortable, and there is no call to court any form of martyrdom in the noble cause of purging the world of stupid and harmful superstitions. Most women who have beautiful bodies declare that they would be only too pleased to exhibit them publicly were the practice admitted. Women who do not possess beautiful bodies are equally averse to subversive standards. But what is demanded by the interests of a healthier morality is not that clothes should be abolished, but that they should cease to be tabus. Nudity is permissible and habitual at the seaside in Sweden, and I am not aware that sexual relations are more disorderly in Sweden than in England.

The regulation of sex relations presents one of the most complex and difficult problems of the modern world. But the sinister farce of Comstockery and Jixity has nothing whatever to do with the regulation of sexual relations, except to poison the sources from which they spring, and there is no problem in regard to them but the problem of human stupidity. It is not, however, because they are ineffably stupid and intolerably vexatious that they are most objectionable, but because they are pestilently harmful. Harmful in the very sense in which they profess to be beneficial. On that account they are things to be opposed, to be fought tooth and nail.

VIII

SEXUAL VALUES

IN one respect the traditional Christian theory upon which moral censorship is founded is, it must be admitted, sound. It assumes that sexual conduct cannot be controlled unless sexual values are also controlled; it postulates the dependence of the one upon the others. The blundering and sex-obsessed Christian Fathers were in so far more realistic than the sex-protected, and therefore intellectualistic Greeks. The latter, who always regarded sexual indulgence as of the same nature as indulgence in food and drink, overlooked an important difference. The misconception is perpetuated in the notion of many intelligent modern persons that sexual manifestations are essentially physiological, and may be regarded as similar to functions of excretion. The biological fact is overlooked that sexual functions are never purely physiological; they are invariably psycho-physiological. That is why the problems of sex, apart from their social aspects, are not problems of hygiene, but of life. In animals sexual reproduction cannot take place as an exclusively physiological function; it demands the condition of rut, that is, the concupiscent, libidinous, lecherous values to which it gives rise. Abolish these, and you abolish the physiological process of sexual reproduction. That physiological process can never be " pure," if by that is meant the elimination of rut and of the psychological values which constitute the sexual attitude.

The Christian theory that in order to suppress sex

" impurity " must be suppressed, and that consequently not only must sexual conduct be repressed, but likewise all sexual values in thought, literature, art, is thus in principle correct. For that very reason the theory is absolutely incompatible with any view of sexual behaviour except that which it was intended to impose, namely, that sex should be obliterated altogether. The only logical term of the stigmatization of sexual values and functions as " impure," " base," " vile," " sinful," is their entire abolition. That was, in fact, the avowed intention of the founders of Christian morality. They did not aim at controlling or regulating, but at obliterating. They were not concerned with safeguarding the institution of marriage, but on the contrary with abolishing it. Their stigmatization of sex was perfectly logical so long as that object was in view. It becomes hopelessly illogical from the moment that any kind of compromise is introduced. As soon as the logically uncompromising view that sex is unmitigated evil, that it is the abomination of abominations, that it must be completely stamped out, is qualified by the Pauline concession that the evil and the abomination must needs be conditionally tolerated as necessary, that necessary evil, which retains the values of baseness, vileness, impurity, sinfulness, becomes a state, not of logical contradiction merely, but of irreconcilable psychological conflict. That hopelessly illogical situation has accordingly had far more serious consequences on the life of Western culture than logical fallacies. For sex being psycho-physiological, you cannot play ducks and drakes with its values without affecting its psycho-physiology.

The consequence to the modern Western world of the Christian theory and its values and of the conflict with its illogical compromises is not bad logic, but bad health, mental and physical.

The sexophobic dementia, the archaic mythologies of third-century Christianity, have evaporated from the intelligent modern mind. But they have left behind them a deposit of values, their damnatory, vituperative values, the " slime," which, in the language of Puritanism and of post-Puritan tradition, is the denotative symbol of the baseness and vileness of sex.

I recall a posthumous page in the *Journal* of Amiel, the Genevese idealist dreamer, which contains his reflections upon his first belated *bonne fortune*—an utterly joyless one. The poor fellow is borne down with spiritual uneasiness and disillusion, and his reflections are an illustration of the text: " *Omne animale post coitum triste.*" " Can it be," he says in effect (I am quoting from memory), " that men will jeopardize and sacrifice so much for *that*? " As the reviewer in the *Times Literary Supplement* very clearly pointed out, the unhappy philosopher was obviously pathetically unaware that what he set down to the nature of things was purely and simply the direct effect of his Calvinistic upbringing, and of nothing else. Common sense might have told him that men and women in all ages have most certainly not sacrificed and jeopardized their all for such a miserable, wilted, diseased thing as Calvinistic values have made of sex. Post-coital sadness is not a phenomenon of natural history, but of Christian pathology.

By imparting baseness to sex, Christian evaluations have to some extent succeeded in their purpose. The traditional evaluation has sunk so deep into the marrow of Western culture, in countries of Puritan tradition at least, that, like bodily pudicity, it mimics a natural phenomenon. The emancipated intelligentsia of England, who strive bewildered in the toils of that tradition, are Puritans. They think Puritan thoughts as M. Jourdain spoke prose. D. H. Lawrence was as thorough a Puritan as Bernard Shaw. H. G. Wells, Arnold Bennett, Aldous Huxley are Puritans. Despite their efforts to be pagan, they are oppressed with the solemn Puritan uneasiness about sex. A most intelligent modern woman, Lady Rhondda, finds no difficulty in making the amazing assertion that " every decent person is a Puritan." Perhaps I am one myself. The effects of infantile religious education are, like those of syphilis, never completely eliminated from the system. Puritan tradition, combined with the Christian management of adolescence, has converted the sexual life of civilized men and women into a neurosis.

A variety of that Puritan deformation is the notion that it can be remedied by reversing Puritan Christian values. Instead of being " base," " vile," " ignoble," " impure," sexual values are to be made " noble," " beautiful," " sublime," " pure." That metamorphosis is, of course, supposed in Christian theory, in the Puritan variety of it more particularly, to be brought about by the sacrament of Holy Matrimony. Puritan rebels against Puritanism commonly aspire to imitating the thaumaturgic achievement by a transubstantiation of Puritan values. The feat of transvaluation proceeds, of course, upon the assumption that what is to be made noble and sublime is in itself base and ignoble. It assumes the Christian values. The sublimation of sex is but a variation on the Christian vilification of sex. The pathetic antics of the modern sublimers of sex reproduce the bewildered perplexity of the early Christian endeavour to reduce the compromise with Satan to the minimum demanded by the physiological requirements of procreation. The emancipated Puritan is obsessed with the enterprise of keeping sex " clean "—which, I presume, means turning off the light.

Whether sex be enslimed in negative or enshrined in positive values, the result is precisely the same. The psycho-physiological effect of suffusing sex with moralistic values, positive or negative, is similar to that described by Rousseau when he tried to combine love with mathematics. " *Lascia le donne e studia le matematiche!* " Moralistic values, baseness or nobility, have as much to do with the psycho-physiological functions of sex as mathematics. The effect of the combination is, in fact, the disease of the age. As a result of it modern men and women are sexual valetudinarians.

The infection of the emotional life with moralistic values has in post-Puritanical cultures begot a secret and shameful disease which is spreading like a plague over those cultures. It made its appearance when the French Revolution compelled the immoral ruling classes to capitulate to bourgeois ideals by adopting bourgeois moralistic values. The Puritan Byron, bred in the midst of Aberdonian Presbyterianism, prostrated under the sense of sin, shocked and infuriated by the discovery of the fact that women possess biological functions, affords the earliest historical instance of the hitherto unknown blighting malady. The sexual palsy of Puritan culture is far from constituting the triumph of the Christian plan for obliterating sex. The effects of the surgical sterilizations which the ancient Christians favoured would be vitalizing compared to the devitalization and unhappiness of which their victims do not know the cause. One finds it actually assumed in Puritan civilization that the consummation of the sexual functions in joint fruition, regarded as normal in every culture of pagan tradition, is exceptional. A literature even exists upon the controversy as to whether the fault lies with men or with women, the fact being, of course, that it lies with both. The erotic infantilism of English men and women is a byword in Latin countries. The anthropologically debated question whether the condition of frigidity, or feminine impotence, is atavistic, is disposed of by ethnological evidence. It is wholly unknown in savage races; it appears to be equally unheard of, or at most exceptional, in non-Puritan countries.

An incidental manifestation of post-Puritan feminine sexophobia is the undoubted spread, in England at least, of tribadism. Miss Radclyffe Hall's novel, *The Well of Loneliness*, sheds an interesting light on the phenomenon. Running through it is the assumption, urged as a plea for tolerance, that the perversion is physiological, the result of a constitutional abnormality, a supposed " excess of masculinity." But it is as clear as day from the document itself that this is a delusion. The cause is not physiological, but cultural, and lies in the frustration of normal erotic functions by the palsy induced by Puritan sexual values, and in the desperate quest for diverted satisfaction in relations emancipated from sexual antagonism and maintained, as the victim supposes, " noble " and " pure " by being uncontaminated with the grossness, vileness, and " adolescent " impurity of masculine urges.

The outlook on sex differs completely in Catholic countries from that prevalent in countries of Puritan tradition. The difference is not, as is constantly supposed, racial, but cultural. Catholicism has long been compelled to come to terms with paganism. When the Puritan Reformation took place Catholicism was in a fair way to becoming indistinguishable from paganism. One of the unfortunate results of the Reformation was to arrest that evolution and to revive the moral zeal of Catholic paganism. At the present day the strange spectacle is witnessed of strutting little Fascist countries, like Italy or Hungary, aping the virtues of Puritan civilization by regulating the length of women's skirts and placing the police in charge of morality. It is quite possible that Puritan sexual valetudinarianism may in time extend to countries of Catholic tradition. So far, however, it has not. Healthy pagan realism has resisted Puritan valetudinarianism. The pagan tradition is considerably older than the Puritan. It is older than Christianity, and Catholic Christianity was quite early in its career obliged to bow to the hereditary prepotence of pagan tradition, and to adopt its moral outlook as it adopted its gods and goddesses disguised as saints and madonnas. What cultural

H

superiority crudely magical, absolutist, and obscurantist Catholicism appears to enjoy over pseudo-rationalistic Protestantism is due to its essentially pagan cultural tradition. The sinfulness of sex is in Catholic countries viewed as part of the original and general sinfulness of human nature, which ranks as a theological dogma having little more real bearing upon the realities of life than other theological dogmas, such as that of the mystery of the Trinity or of the immaculate conception. The sinfulness of human nature is provided for by ritual absolution. That lustral function, equivalent to the Athenian Myrrhine's ablution in the water-clock, is the express function and chief utility of religion. " *C'est son métier*." And the purity preserved by means of ritual lustration is the pagan ritual purity, not the Puritan moralistic, self-righteous purity. Catholic religion is ritualistic, not like Evangelical religion, moralistic. Ritual provisions for the remission of sin are of more importance than moral provisions for its prevention.

The impurity of sex, like every other consequence of the Fall, that is, like every other fact of life, is in the pagan tradition of Catholic countries susceptible of being viewed, like any other abstract theological dogma, lightly, jocularly, humorously. It has not the tremendous portentousness of Puritan moral earnestness. Puritanism, like Hebraism, is incapable of humour. What the French and Nietzsche call " *la niaiserie anglaise*," English imbecility, is the Puritan infinite capacity for lack of humour. The most devout Catholic is able to abstract the humorous and joyous aspect of sex, as of any other fact of life, without any sense of grossness or salacity. To the Puritan such " Gallic wit "—nowise " Gallic," but pagan —is the most infuriating and scandalous of depravities. Sin is to him no joking matter. Nor is it to the " emancipated " post-Puritan, who is earnestly intent upon " uplifting " sex and making it " pure " and " noble." Puritan *niaiserie* is summed up in countries of pagan culture by the term " shocking," which stands for an attitude unintelligible and strangely uncivilized to pagan mentality. A French or Italian duchess could not conceive such a lapse of good manners as to profess to be " shocked." To her mind the " shocked " Victorian *grande dame* is behaving like a peasant. What the Puritan accounts immodesty, betokening deplorable moral corruption, is viewed by the pious, chaste, and utterly modest Catholic lady who laughs over a salacious tale, in the light of humour. She may, on grounds of chastity and modesty, object to sex, but if she accepts it, she is not concerned with endowing it with extraneous values, positive or negative. If she makes love, she is not concerned with being " pure " and " noble." The sexual emotions retain in countries of pagan tradition their own values, their pagan character of joy. They have not become invalided through the sense of sin. Puritan psycho-physiological valetudinarianism, which arises from the conflict between irreconcilable values, is totally impossible to the most modest, inexpert, and unsophisticated Italian, Spanish, French, or Flemish virgin. It would never occur to her to endeavour to transvaluate sexual values, or to formulate any. No European man or woman who has not been indoctrinated by Puritan *niaiserie* has ever asked whether sex be base or noble. Sex, whether base or noble, has accordingly remained healthy, which is the only value applicable to the category of psycho-physiological functions.

The pseudo-problem which engages the attention of the majority of present-day post-Puritan immoralists, sexologists, and bewildered intelligent men and women, is exactly similar to the pseudo-problem of police moral censorship—where to " draw the line." They are concerned with purifying sexual values, with ennobling them, by " drawing the line " at what, in their post-Puritan tradition, are its baser and more corrupt aspects. The fallacy, both as regards police censorship and the " ennobling " of sexual values, lies in the unapprehended fact that " the line " is automatically drawn by social and cultural conditions themselves, and that no line can be arbitrarily and artificially drawn by the deliberate imposition of values. To draw such a line arbitrarily and artificially is to defeat certainly and surely the very purpose of drawing it. For whatever is excluded by the line drawn becomes at once invested by that very act with a greatly enhanced sexual value. That enhanced sexual value is not the effect of intrinsic " baseness " or of any of the estimates which determine the drawing of the line, but of that line itself, that is, of the state of conflict set up by the imposition of the tabu. It is that conflict itself and nothing else which constitutes the alleged " baseness," and also the resulting valetudinarianism, associated with the excluded aspect. Abolish the line, you thereby automatically abolish what you vaguely sought to exclude by drawing it. The line draws itself. Draw a line by censorship or moralistic values; you preserve what you proposed to obliterate. The " ennobling " and " purifying " of sex, in so far as the enterprise possesses any meaning, consist in suppressing conflicting values, not in imposing arbitrary ones. Sexual evaluations can only be made more healthy by abolishing psychological conflicts. The effect of imposing extraneous and irrelevant values upon sex has never had any bearing upon morality of any kind; it has merely been to produce sexual valetudinarianism.

The Christian baseness and impurity of sex have, in the post-Puritanical deranged mentality, become translated into the depreciation of " functions of excretion." The Christian dualistic mythology of divine soul and vile body is re-edited by a frustrated generation as the reduction of sex to physiology. The frustrated generation's claim to realism should, however, suggest the logical question whether any human phenomenon lies outside the sphere of physiology. Is not the assigning of physiological values to sex by detached intellectual frigidity, itself a physiological phenomenon? Intellectual frigidity pronounces its considered conclusion that a wholly exaggerated, monstrously hypertrophied importance has become assigned to a particular " function of excretion." It is, however, to be frigidly noted that biological realities assign so monstrously hypertrophied an importance to physiological functions that human life consists of nothing else. A monstrous importance is assigned to functions of nutrition. Social humanity's civilized organization rests upon the monstrous importance attached to bread and butter. The physiological operation of a man or woman's peptic glands is not a matter of undue mental excitation so long as his or her bank-manager guarantees the automatic serving of three or four somewhat tedious daily meals, and the doctor finds no occasion to prescribe soda-mints. But the physiological operation of the peptic glands may assume a quite monstrous importance if the bank-manager declines to provide that guarantee. The disturbed functions of the peptic glands may bring about Bolshevism. The frigid intellect of Western civilization is at the present moment solely engaged with anything but frigid concern in the task of preventing disordered peptic glands from blowing it up. The nervously spasmodic dismissal of sex to the category of excretory functions by exasperated frustrates is unadulterated *niaiserie anglaise*. And the post-Puritanical hypocrisy is no advance in realism over Puritanical ignorance of physiology.

The functions of gonadal glands are of no more and no less importance than those of peptic glands. Their functions are no more disturbing or obsessing so long as their operation is normal. The normal operation of peptic or gonadal glands does not interfere in the least with that of any other function, interest, or occupation, physiological, intellectual, emotional, spiritual or ethereally sublimated of the human organism, male or female. But any disturbance in that operation brings about a disturbance in the operation of all other functions, and the disturbance brought about by the gonadal glands is even more profound than that brought about by the peptic glands, and affects the more intellectual, emotional, and spiritual functions to a greater extent than the more physiological. The disastrous thing is that when people's intelligence, emotions, and spiritual functions are hopelessly deranged, they are not aware of it, and quite honestly believe themselves to be normal, and normal people to be in need of conversion. The lunatic calls from behind the asylum wall to an insane world to come in and become sane. The world is full of intellectual and emotional valetudinarians who protest that nothing is the matter with them, and far from being induced to see a doctor, are itching to prescribe for other people.

The preoccupation of the present age with sex, its sexologies, its sex-haunted literature, is the overdue rational revolt against the dogmatic absolutism of traditional tabu values. But it is also the outcome of the devastation wrought by those values and of the creeping general palsy resulting from the incompatible mixture of morals, mathematics, and what-not with sexual values. Moral values have a great deal to do with the relations between the sexes, but they have no more to do with sexual functions than mathematics. The behaviour of men and women towards one another may be noble or ignoble, just or unjust, admirable or despicable. But sexual functions can no more be any of those things than they can be oblong or octahedral. They can, like the functions of the peptic glands, be healthy or diseased. And that is properly the only category of values applicable to sexual functions. The whole distorted perspective created by Christian and post-Christian values is the result of their irrelevance. The question is not whether sex should be regarded as base or noble, whether people should be chaste or unchaste, but whether they should be healthy or morbid. Both continence and lubricity, chastity and unchastity, may be healthy or they may be morbid. As in every other function of life, health and sanity lie in moderate activity. Whether a man or woman is continent or the reverse, his or her sex life will be healthy so long as it is not artificially over-stimulated or over-repressed. And that sexual life will be not only unhealthy, but hopelessly diseased which is at one and the same time unnaturally stimulated and unnaturally repressed. Which is precisely the state of things secured by Puritanical and post-Puritanical values.

The journalese superficiality that the present age is sex-obsessed is, of course, a *niaiserie anglaise* of the first water. The concern with sex shown by the present age is as nothing compared to the frenzied obsession of early Christianity. It is indeed a protest against the nauseating morbidity of Victorian sex-obsession, the ubiquitous pruriency of which went about treading on egg-shells in perpetual alarm lest the existence of sex should be betrayed. It expurgated its medical text-books, spoke a bowdlerized tongue, strewed the world with fig-leaves, enforced purdah upon women, and broke out into epidemics of witch-persecution whenever the breath of scandal blew aside a corner of the veil of its hypocrisy. All Christian culture has been sex-obsessed. Non-Christian cultures, from those of the savage upwards, are, of course, likewise sex-obsessed inasmuch as sex is central in their emotional life, the functions of the gonadal glands being biologically of greater racial importance than those of the peptic glands.

To reduce to a minimum the disturbing influence of sex, which is the professed object of Christian sex-morality, has been the achievement of one people only, the Greeks. The paganism from which Christianity liberated the world came nearer than any other culture to accomplishing what Christianity claimed to accomplish. Greek paganism was in a higher degree than any other culture free from sex-obsession. This in a people who had neither a name for chastity nor a conception of the virtue, was not the outcome of particular principles, but of their general attitude towards life, which was the exact opposite of the Christian's and the Puritan's. Instead of making it their aim to renounce and suppress enjoyment, the Greeks aimed at heightening and cultivating it.

Commenting upon the Greek Anthology, Lafcadio Hearn explained as follows the Greek point of view to his Japanese students. " The Eastern religions, including Christianity, taught that because everything in the world is uncertain, impermanent, perishable, therefore we ought not to allow our minds to love worldly things. But the Greek mind, as expressed by the old epigraphy in the cemeteries, not less than by the teaching of Mimnermus, took exactly the opposite view. ' O children of men, it is because beauty and pleasure and love and light can last only a little while, it is exactly because of this that you should love them. Why refuse to enjoy the present because it cannot last for ever? ' " Hearn goes on to compare that attitude with that of Omar Khayyám. But the Greek view differed as much from that of the Persian pessimist as it did from the Christian's. Omar is an Oriental, and his attitude is allied to that of the Jewish author of *Ecclesiastes*, not to the Greek's. The Greek's philosophy of life was not to make the best of a poor thing, but to appreciate to the utmost a beautiful thing. The Greek was not resigned to life : he was in love with it. But—and that is the whole value of the Greek point of view—his notion of enjoyment was not the barbarian's. The gross Nordic barbarians whom he saw drunk and shouting, and indulging in orgies when they meant to enjoy themselves, filled him with pity and disgust. The Greek's conception of enjoyment and pleasure was to train himself to distil from life its most precious and delicate qualities, to train his senses to catch the most subtle aromas, to extract from common life, from the ordinary circumstances of everyday existence, the quality which in some form or other, in some form ever varied and new, is always there, the quality which makes it a thing of interest and therefore of beauty, an object of love and therefore of enjoyment. That point of view, that conception of enjoyment, of pleasure, is that of the artist; it is the essence of art. The Greek artist, were he to-day brought into the midst of the luxury, the pleasure-seeking of modern civilization, would look upon the notions of enjoyment, of pleasure of the modern barbarian with the same pity and disgust as he did on the drunken orgies of the barbarians of his day. He would have looked with the same contempt upon barbarian vulgarity, empty opulence, frenzied striving for high-pitched stimulation, restless search for strange sensations and excitements, in the twentieth century as he did in the fifth century B.C. The Greek was in doubt whether jewels, bracelets, ear-rings, added to the beauty of the women he admired, or whether they did not rather detract from the perfection of pure form. What would he have thought of the exotic barbarism which is accounted the ideal of sexual attraction by the modern votaries of pleasure?

It was by that general attitude towards life, and not by any repressive and inhibitory principles, that the Greeks were protected, in spite of a quite unsatisfactory sexual organization, from sex-obsession. Sex itself had with them no extraneous and irrelevant values; it was not held to be base and impure, nor was it accounted noble and pure. Sex needs no extraneous and irrelevant values. Social conditions impose limitations and control over its mani-festations, but that control calls for no other means of repression than the demands of those social conditions. As soon as that necessary control borrows spurious and artificial repressing values, the result is the same as when spurious and artificial stimulations are resorted to. The effect in either case is psycho-physiological disease.

IX

THE EMANCIPATION OF WOMEN

THE present tide of criticism and revolt against traditional sex-morality is, as already noted, the inevitable protest of reason against arbitrary dogmatic standards resting upon superstition. But that inevitable revolt has been brought to a head by social causes of fundamental significance. Traditional sexual morality has a double origin. The vehement sexophobia and the fierce damnatory sexual values of early Christianity were the outgrowth of primitive superstitious conceptions of the magic efficiency of mortification. They were originally directed against the institution of marriage no less than against any other form of sexual activity. But sexual restrictions, besides their reference to magical functions, have also arisen in relation to the social organization of sex relations. Those restrictions have been extremely slow in developing. In the lowest phases of social culture individual relations between the sexes impose very few restrictions on the freedom of conduct of either men or women. The claims of men to the exclusive sexual possession of women have developed almost as slowly in primitive societies as the claims to individual property. It is only in relatively advanced social phases, phases where already aristocratic classes have come into existence and private property is an established institution, that the claim to absolute marital ownership is found firmly established. To that claim there becomes added in still more advanced social phases the retrospective claim to the chastity of unmarried girls. Thus has eventually been brought about the standard of feminine virtue which restricts the sexual life of a woman to relations with one man.

From the nature and purpose of the restrictive standard it is applicable to women only. This is taken for granted in the majority of civilized societies, the virtue of men being left out of account. The Christian tradition incorporated the patriarchal tradition of feminine chastity, and professedly regarded it as a particular aspect of the doctrine of chastity as a substantial virtue. Chastity and purity are in the Christian theory independent of sex and equally applicable as a moral requirement to both. But that theoretical subsumption of feminine chastity under the conception of the moral merit of chastity in general has by no means obliterated the fundamental difference in origin and purpose between the two traditions. However vehemently the values of Christian morality may be emphasized, a radical difference which nothing has been able to efface entirely, has persisted throughout Western tradition in the application of those values to men and to women respectively. Chastity, purity, modesty are in that tradition regarded as special feminine virtues. In harmony with a method of interpretation universally applied in such cases, the notion has become established that those " feminine " virtues are natural and more deeply seated in the very constitution of women than in that of men. The claim that women ought to be more chaste and pure than men has, by a curious evolution, given rise to the belief that they are, in fact, by nature more chaste

and pure. Women themselves have been deeply influenced
by that naïve piece of sophistry. They have become
persuaded that while they are by nature and innate disposition endowed with sexual impulses of an elevated and
sublimated type, men are, by their congenital disposition,
gross and impure. From being forcibly compelled to be
chaste, women came first to be regarded as naturally chaste,
and by the insistent pressure of that opinion came at last
to regard an imputation of unchastity or impurity as a
slander against their natural disposition. It was the
Victorian theory that the " public morals " enforced by
the police were chiefly intended to protect the delicate
susceptibility of women against lesions to their feelings,
and it is still the vague notion of Jixity that it derives
its chief inspiration from reverence for womanhood. The
perfect culmination of savage masculine claims to exclusive
sexual proprietorship was reached in China and Victorian
England. A purity implying complete ignorance of the
facts of physiology and of life, a modesty whose exquisite
sensitiveness was incommodated by an allusion to ankles,
were associated in that ideal of perfect womanhood with
the gentleness of absolute submission and subserviency to
masculine superiority in Katay and in the Grand Siècle of
Bourgeois England.

What is termed the emancipation of modern woman,
however lightly and jocularly regarded and however
superficial it may be accounted, constitutes in fact one of
the most profound and radical revolutions which has taken
place within historical times. Social and political upheavals
like the French Revolution or the Great War have had

direct consequences on the social and political order merely. The change brought about by the emancipation of women is almost biological. It bears, at any rate, on the biological foundations of the constitution of society. Nothing of the kind has ever taken place before in historical societies. Throughout all social, political, religious changes and revolutions, historical societies have remained patriarchal. The emancipation of women which in its overt aspect seemed to be no more than a paltry extension of the parliamentary franchise, the most trifling and insignificant of changes in an insignificant political machinery, means in effect the breaking down of the patriarchal constitution of society.

With the collapse into obsolescence of the patriarchal principle upon which half the sexual morality of Western tradition was founded, the entire structure has inevitably become transferred from the pedestal of unquestionable categorical authority implanted by nature in the human conscience to the dust of the arena of criticism. Women cannot repudiate the patriarchal convention of their subordination to masculine claims without at the same time repudiating the patriarchal convention of the special applicability to them of the virtues of chastity, modesty, and purity. Christian traditional morality is not primarily founded upon that convention; it is founded upon the sinfulness of all manifestations of sex. But the necessary compromise which ascetic Christian sexophobia has been forced to accept has rested upon the patriarchal convention, and the purpose of sex-morality from being the complete obliteration of sex has, in Western tradition, come to be understood as the safeguarding of the sanctity of patriarchal marriage. With the repudiation of the patriarchal subordination of women, with the repudiation of Chinese and Victorian ideals of perfect and perfectly subordinated womanhood, the whole edifice of traditional Western sexual morality collapses from its immemorial pedestal into the melting-pot.

It is an amazing illustration of the ostrich-policy rigorously observed in all that has reference to sex-morals that the inevitable logical consequence was not perceived. When the suffragettes were supplying the comic papers with a windfall by their agitation for a right to vote at parliamentary elections about which few people cared two straws, neither they nor anyone else suspected that the venerable edifice of Christian morality was being jeopardized. Most people are quite incapable even at the present hour of perceiving the inexorable logical nexus. That is because their minds are stuffed with fantastic fables on the subject, because they have not the vaguest notion of the facts of cultural history or of the origin of moral ideas, and have been in the habit of believing that the latter consist in eternal laws inscribed by nature on the human conscience. That those eternal laws should have anything to do with votes for women sounds manifestly preposterous.

The present signs of disturbance in the eternal laws are, our press columnists and smarty-smart professional pooh-poohers will explain, nothing more serious than a passing reaction against the well-meant, but perhaps slightly overdone prudery of Victorian tradition. They will cite periods of similar reaction and have wise things to say about the swing of pendulums. And after all—" after all " is an expression which never fails to impress the British public, affording as it does a sense of moderation and an appeal to the " British genius for compromise "— after all, any departure which is to be noted from the eternal principles embodied in Victorian codes is a phenomenon confined to a negligibly small, if much written-up section of modern womanhood. For the vast majority of English and American womanhood the eternal principles remain as much in force as ever. Numerical statistics of opinions have, however, very little to do with such matters. Evolutionary changes of opinion do not depend on numerical statistics; they depend on logic. Every change of opinion is represented during the critical stages of its development by negligible numerical minorities. But the revolutions of human opinion are not determined by a count of heads. Women who are emancipated from patriarchal principles may cherish an abundance of muddle-headed and absurd ideas, but their change of attitude on the question has four-square logic on its side. If the special applicability of moral values to women rests upon the patriarchal theory of their subordination, then that special applicability cannot survive the repudiation of their subordination. Neither numbers nor the swing of fashion nor any amount of adventitious silliness has any bearing upon the rough logic of the situation. It is having such rough four-square logic on their side that people used to call having God on their side. And there is not the slightest parallel or analogy between re-

I

actions against Puritan tyranny under the Commonwealth, such as the reaction of the Restoration, and the logic arising out of the situation brought about by the recognition of women's claims to civic and political equality. The fatuous assurance that the reconsideration of principles of sexual morality at the present day is a passing whim is mere ostrich-policy. It is not the swinging of a capricious pendulum, but the rocking of the entire edifice of moral values inherited by Western culture.

The logical consequences of the emancipation of women are far more serious and perplexing than the logical consequences of anthropological knowledge concerning the origin of tabus. With regard to the latter there cannot be two opinions—though of course there are, human stupidity being particularly pertinacious where tabus are concerned. The scrapping of superstitious tabus can have no more effect on moral conduct than their observance. It does not make the slightest difference to the structure of human society that the stationer round the corner sells Parisian postcards. The sanitary effect of the scrapping of superstitious tabus, which would render the stationer's postcards unsaleable, cannot be other than beneficial. But the revolt of women against patriarchal principles is another matter. It involves not merely the standards by which policemen, police magistrates, Home Secretaries, and Shoe Lane journalists shall be guided in the task of protecting women's morals, but the standards by which the relations between the sexes shall be regulated, that is to say, the very structure of civilized society. The structure of civilized society would not be in the least affected by the sale of

James Joyce's works on every bookstall, but it would be affected by women's refusal to recognize patriarchal principles. The scrapping of tabus only affects sexual values, the scrapping of patriarchal principles affects sexual behaviour.

The suffragettes who asked for the vote and got it went, then, very much farther than the obscene novelists or the German nudists. While obscene literature and public nudity are really entirely innocuous, female suffrage, which people regard as quite reasonable and proper, is really a far more horribly subversive enormity. Most of the women who demanded the abolition of monosexual legislation would have been scared out of their wits if anyone had demanded the abolition of clothes, and most women who vote are quite unconscious of the fact that, while it would not make the slightest difference, so far as the social order is concerned, if they went to the polling-booth naked, their voting at all strikes at the very roots of that social order.

It is precisely such bottomless ignorance which makes the distasteful discussion of sex necessary at the present day. I heartily sympathize with all objections against that discussion. Sex is no more a proper subject for discussion than it is a subject for mathematics. I entirely agree with the Victorians; they did not discuss, they merely did. That is why, despite their abominable vices, they were more healthy than the present discussing generation. When people protest against sex-obsession taking the form of thrashing out the inextricable dilemmas of the situation in which we are landed, instead of observing, like the

Victorians, the tabus of complete silence which lent such heightened charm to surreptitious lechery, I can quite understand their squeamishness. Victorian indecency has had to be sacrificed to the obstetric task thrust upon the world by the women, of bringing into existence reconsidered standards of morals. The indecent discussion must continue until the Augean stable of misconceptions and ignorance left by pre-emancipation morality is sufficiently clear to house adequate moral ideas.

The enormous difficulties of the task imposed upon the world by women are increased by the circumstance that it cannot be carried out without their co-operation. It is not the stupidity and ignorance of University professors which has to be dissipated before light can penetrate, but the irrationalities and ignorances which are lodged in the charming heads of the women themselves. They have done the mischief by asking for the right to record their votes at political elections, without perceiving the inevitable consequences of their innocent fun. Political and civic equality of the sexes implies moral equality. It implies the perfectly appalling logical consequence that the morals of women shall in future be the same as those of a respectable Christian Victorian man—at best. That, of course, means the total collapse of Christian morality. If the standards of Christian morality are to be observed by women in the same manner as they have for the last two thousand years been observed by men, there is an end to Christian morality. And the matter is made still more hopeless by the fact that the decision as to what standards of morality shall be observed can no longer be dictated by men; it lies in the hands of women. Patriarchal and Pauline principles have been repudiated by them, not because of the intrinsic merits or demerits of those principles, but because they assumed the right of men to dictate the standards of feminine morality. Accordingly professorial and philosophic discussion of the matter and ecclesiastical pronouncements and pastorals are only valid so far as they succeed in convincing the women.

The pathetic delusion that present-day revolt against traditional tabu-morality is a passing whim of fashion is as struthious as the supposition that it is a manifestation of licentiousness. Whether its ultimate outcome is greater licentiousness or more austere sexual control depends entirely upon the persuasive powers of the appeal that can be made to intelligent modern women. It does not depend upon the reaffirmation of the divine authority of tabus. Thus the most momentous moral revolution that has taken place since the introduction of Christianity is an accomplished fact; the categorical authority of coercive imperatives is deposed, and can never be reinstated while civilization lasts. No dogmatic, autocratic, absolutist, categorical authority ever does survive the first slap in the face which it receives. The partisans of deceased absolutism may contrive new petty tyrannies, strutting Fascisms, impudent bullyings aping deceased majesty, but the charmed spell of right divine once gone is gone for ever. For it there is no resurrection. Categorical moral imperatives graven by nature in the human heart, unquestioned and unquestionable, refusing to be argued with, have in the present year of grace taken up their abode in the limbo of scrapped obsoleteness because women are no longer content to recognize the divine categorical nature of the " virtue " dictated by patriarchal principles. The tremendous revolution is not affected by the fact that millions of men and women have not yet heard that it has taken place. Nor can the patriarchal principles which have for thousands of years been regarded by both men and women as axiomatic recover the axiomatic force of which they have been divested by the emancipation of women.

X

MARRIAGE AND BIOLOGY

THE revolution brought about by the emancipation of women has, like all revolutions, created derangements in a hitherto orderly world. So long as the divinely or naturally appointed authority of patriarchal principles went undisputed, things went on smoothly. Women were the most fervent upholders of those principles. They were duly pure, exquisitely shockable, conscientiously tender and submissive, religiously dutiful, angelically patient, and everything went merrily as a marriage bell. There were, no doubt, abundant tragedies and miseries, crushed lives, loveless homes. But those tragedies and sufferings were set down to the natural cruelty of life; they were endured by women in the spirit of patient fortitude with which, with the invaluable aid of the comforts and consolations of religion, one submits to life's hardships. That heroic fortitude, that Griselda-like patience, that divine sweetness which constituted the supreme charm of the ideal Victorian woman, have of necessity become more rare, and are likely to become rarer. Such is the inevitable result when the words " justice " and " right " come to be uttered more often than the word " duty."

One of the most pronounced effects of women's claim to equality with men has been to accentuate enormously the inequality between men and women. There is, of course, inequality between the sexes. Sex, biologically and anatomically, means that. Sexual differences cannot be entirely obliterated by orange juice. No reducing diet or ingeniously constructed corsets can do away entirely with the differences which constitute sex. In fact, the circumstance which imparts to sex its disturbing anti-social character, the fact which suggested the invectives of the Christian Fathers and the plan to abolish sex, is that no form of social organization, no system of moral principles, no religion and no Act of Parliament can do away with biological facts. Civilized humanity, with its stately cities and empires, its sciences and its arts, its aeroplanes and radios, is a mighty and wonderful achievement. But for all that it ultimately rests just as much on biological facts as do pigs and oysters. Do what you will you cannot get away from biology. Fundamental biological facts can no more be obliterated by orange juice and dry toast than by Christian moral doctrines.

Biology is the foundation. Logically it should be the foundation of any system of education. Unfortunately it is not. The erudite Dean Inge, who would be suffused with unsurvivable shame were he found guilty of having perpetrated a false Greek accent, is not in the least embarrassed when repeating the old howler that gorillas live respectable family lives. Complete ignorance of biology, which, of course, does not exclude the right to found scholarly arguments on biological howlers, is quite consistent with the highest academic attainments. The modern intelligent woman is learned in psychology, sociology, anthropology. But all that learning of the modern intelligent woman is inadequate if her biology is shaky. She need not be ashamed of her ignorance any more than Dean Inge is ashamed of his. It is shared by the professors who teach her psychology, sociology, and anthropology. It is even to a large extent shared by the biologists themselves.

The reason is a very significant and important one. The inviolable authority of traditional moral tabus and patriarchal principles has not only imposed itself upon general current ideas, social standards, legislation, literature, art; it has also imposed itself upon science. Victorian text-books of physiology omitted any reference to sexual functions, so that they might be read in Victorian drawing-rooms. Victorian text-books of psychology were equally beseeming in regard to sexual emotions. No very serious harm has resulted from that pudicity of physiologists and psychologists. But considerable mischief and confusion have resulted when the moral sentiments of men of science, instead of manifesting themselves in discreet silence and pudibond bowdlerization, have led them to invent whole accounts of their sciences evolved from the depths of their traditional moral consciences. That is what has been done with great success and applause in the case of social anthropology, for instance. In the Victorian age some indiscreet scholars had the shameless effrontery to attempt to inquire into the history of traditional moral institutions, and founded the science of social anthropology by gathering together and systematizing the available information concerning the habits and manners of uncivilized and un-Christian humanity. The result was scandalous. It actually presented a clear history of the origin and development of patriarchal marriage. This was an obscenity not to be tolerated. Unfortunately the text-books of the founders of scientific anthropology could not be seized by the police under the Obscene Publications Act of 1857 or under the Blasphemy Laws. A new school of anthropological professors was imported from remote lands into English universities to put a stop to the scandal and to safeguard the sanctity of patriarchal marriage by proving, with many more notes and references than the indiscreet pioneers of the indecent science, the traditional and beseeming Adam-and-Eve version of the history of marriage.

We have not yet come down to the brass-tacks of biology. The authors of the Adam-and-Eve history of marriage felt that some biological background was appropriate—owing to the new disturbing doctrines of evolution, and in order to account for the marriage of Adam and Eve—and being entirely innocent of biology, they found that appropriate background in the story of Noah's Ark. They were not altogether to blame for their naïve biology, for the biologists themselves gave them little help. They were too busy with gametes, chromosomes, genes, determinants of heredity, to have much time to attend to the operation of the functions of reproduction in animals. That department was generally understood not to appertain to the business of the biologist, and was left to various amateurs who dabbled in " natural history," in the same manner as anthropology had long been left to missionaries and rum-traders. In precisely the same manner as missionaries and rum-traders started their anthropological studies by assuming the Adam-and-Eve tradition, so the naturalists set out on their nature-study on the assumption of Noah's Ark biology.

I have personally incurred a good deal of odium and academic scorn for venturing to question the story of Noah's Ark and that of Adam and Eve. In spite of the admittedly unsatisfactory character of our materials, which consists in the one case of the observations of missionaries and rum-traders, and in the other of the observations of naturalists, it is quite possible with a little patience and judgment to get at the facts. And the facts are that animals do not as a rule go two by two, and that savages do not hold adequate views concerning the sanctity of monogamic marriage. One naturalist, a certain Charles Darwin, pointed out the fact that all animals, even those which are occasionally seen at the season of rut going two by two, become completely promiscuous the moment the opportunity offers. The intelligent man or woman who has not the time to go in the jungle and observe the habits of animals, and who is at the mercy of moral professors, can form, nevertheless, a fair opinion concerning the sexual habits of domestic dogs and cats. It is a mistake to suppose that the morals of those animals are corrupted by civilization. They are no more affected by civilization than by the story of Noah's Ark, and the patient observer who goes to the jungle to discover some confirmation of the story of Noah's Ark finds that he could have obtained all the information he wanted by sitting in his backyard. He finds that the habits of cats and dogs in Africa or India are identical with those of cats and dogs in London, and that other animals, such as monkeys and gorillas, show no advance in Christian and patriarchal principles of morality over tabby-cats. Far from there existing any disposition in the sexes to associate two by two, there is, on the contrary, a very constant and conspicuous disposition for them to avoid one another like poison. Male and female animals are impelled to seek one another only at such time as they are under the influence of rut. The female, inspired by a masochistic instinct, then submits to being mawled and mangled by the male, and the male is inspired by a sadistic instinct to attack the female and sometimes to kill her. The attraction between the sexes has reference, among mammalian animals, exclusively to that brutal encounter, and not to any disposition to go two by two and to set up housekeeping. The superficial appearance of such a disposition during the hatching season in birds, among whom the male is specially interested in eggs, is quite deceptive and irrelevant and has no bearing on the sexual reactions of mammalian animals, which do not lay eggs. Noah's Ark biology is as destitute of foundation as Adam-and-Eve anthropology. Both are the outcome, not of scientific observation, but of the established tradition of Christian and patriarchal morality.

The bearing of biological facts on the views of modern emancipated woman is not to seduce her into adopting the morals of tabby-cats, but to throw light upon the assumption that marriage is natural. For a male and a female to live continuously together is, on the contrary, biologically speaking, an extremely unnatural condition. And there do not accordingly exist any biological provisions or adaptations calculated to facilitate the process. Ignorance of biology, and the consequent defenceless aptitude to swallow, like Dean Inge, the story of Noah's Ark, has been one of the most common and important causes of marriage disasters. Quite intelligent men and women contract marriages under the impression that once those marriages are made in heaven or at the Register Office, nature, or natural biological dispositions will look after the rest. They imagine and have indeed been expressly told by the " classic " authorities on the subject that they possess natural dispositions for cohabiting until death do them part, and that those natural dispositions will operate automatically without their taking the slightest trouble about the natural mechanism. The appalling wreckage of human lives which is the outcome of those fantastic views is beyond computation. Classic authorities on the history of human marriage have more to answer for than Spanish Grand Inquisitors. Their hands are imbrued with blood and tears.

Another important consequence of biological facts is that the two sexes are not, and cannot be, as regards their sexual dispositions, equal. The modern intelligent woman who shook her head approvingly over the last paragraph, will here stiffen her neck and disapprove. Nevertheless it is a biological fact that the two sexes differ not only in anatomical peculiarities which cannot be obliterated by orange juice, but in the functions corresponding to those anatomical differences. Biological function, be it explained in order to avoid misunderstandings, is not the same thing as conscious purpose, intention, or desire. All living organisms are elaborately adapted to perform biological functions, but they are commonly not in the least interested in the biological results of performing those functions. The function of sexual activity is to perpetuate the race, but neither animals nor men and women are in the least concerned with the perpetuation of the race when they engage in sexual activities. The biological function, then, of the female's sexual activity is to get herself impregnated. It is not, as has been supposed, to found a home, to obtain the protection of a man or access to his banking account. For despite the edifying misrepresentations of Noah's Ark biology, there exists no instance among the higher animals of males protecting or assisting females. Noah's Ark biology is merely a crude anthropomorphic mythology produced by translating into terms of natural history the patriarchal female's dependence upon her husband's banking account. That banking account is a tremendous attraction to the woman in a civilized patriarchal society, but it does, nevertheless, not belong to the sphere of biological facts. Further, it is no advantage to the biological functions of a woman to have sexual relations with many men. That is, indeed, probably disadvantageous. A woman can bear a child only once a year. All that is necessary therefore to fulfil to the utmost the requirements of her biological functions is to have intercourse once a year.

The biological functions of the male are quite different. Their aim is to impregnate as many females as possible. The male animal wanders in search of females; the animal female seeks a secluded shelter where she can perform her functions of brooding. The male animal who has access to one or more females at once neglects them to impregnate a new female; the animal female who has been impregnated at once avoids all males and resents their presence.

Those are some of the fundamental functional differences between males and females. They involve many more. Indeed every function, and every fibre, and every cell of the male is constituted after a masculine pattern; and every function, every fibre, and every cell of the female is feminine. A woman's handwriting is clearly distinguishable from a man's; a woman's printed writing differs equally from a man's. Every movement of her fingers and every motion of her grey matter is feminine.

Biological functions have of necessity to be adapted to social life, which is not biological. The economic association of men and women is not biological; in nature every individual animal, male or female, fends for itself. The strong pressure of economic requirements which induces a woman to seek an economic protector with a banking account, and constitutes one of the most important inducements to marriage, is not biological. It does not appertain to the sphere of biology, but to that of propertied society. The animal female does not seek a protector or economic helper, but a male that shall impregnate her. When it is assumed that economic cohabitation is a biological state of things, provided for by natural dispositions, by the natural attraction between the sexes, that stupendous fallacy is more mythical than any theological improbability against which modern intelligence revolts. What is taught in Sunday Schools is accurate, historical, and scientific compared with what is taught in Universities and learned societies devoted to the study of Adam-and-Eve anthropology and Noah's

Ark biology. It is, unfortunately, not science merely which suffers, but the man and woman in the street and in the home.

If the history of the institution of marriage be adequately followed up, it is found that from its very inception in the most uncultured societies down to the present stage of civilization, it rests not upon biological or functional, or natural facts, but upon economic and social dispositions. The Australian black, when asked why he marries, answers quite naturally and without any subtle theoretical preconceptions, that he takes a wife in order to have a woman to cook for him and to attend to his household arrangements generally. He does not say that he marries her because he loves her or because he requires her for the satisfaction of his sexual appetites. Both those reasons would be absurd; the first because he has no notion of what we understand by love, the second because there is not the slightest need for him to marry a woman in order to satisfy his sexual appetites. He does not say that he marries her because he would like to have children, for, although he is fonder of children than the majority of English fathers, children are in his society regarded first and foremost as members of the tribe, or as we should say, they belong to the State, and they are not heirs to his estate or his family name.

If, following the various forms of the institution of marriage, we work our way up from the Australian black through every form of low or advanced culture, through the matrimonial arrangements of African chiefs and those of Chinese mandarins, to those of a French aristocrat or a French peasant, we shall find that the transaction, in every quarter of the globe and in every age, rests chiefly, and in most instances exclusively, upon economic considerations. The sordid economic considerations which intrude upon the romance of Edwin and Angelina, and take a good deal of the gilt off the romantic gingerbread even before the raptures of the honeymoon, are not adventitious intrusions, but are everywhere a predominant feature of the arrangement. The reason why the French or English aristocrat marries is not quite the same as that for which the French peasant or the Australian black marries. The noble duke does not require a duchess in order that she should cook his dinner or gather firewood, but he requires her in order that he should have an heir to inherit the family property and carry on the family name and tradition. (For the family is the foundation of society.) The economic anxiety which mars Edwin and Angelina's rapturous idyll, and not those raptures themselves, constitute the reality of the arrangement into which they enter.

The sanctity of patriarchal marriage, which it is one of the professed purposes of traditional morality to safeguard, belongs to a somewhat different order of facts from that of the abstract merit of purity and chastity. It belongs to the order of economic facts. That circumstance is disguised by the ancient custom of concluding that economic transaction in a church. When a considerable amount of property was at stake, the ancient Romans went to a priest to have the marriage contract sworn in due form, because priests amongst them carried out the duties of Commissioners of Oaths. The Christian Church pronounces a blessing on a union on which it formerly pronounced a curse. The con-

K

fusion to which professors of anthropology have so learnedly contributed is thus made worse confounded by making it appear that marriage is concerned with religion and morality, whereas it is concerned with property. Properly speaking, the ceremony of patriarchal marriage should be conducted not by the vicar, but by the bank-manager. Those rationalists who, repudiating the extreme view that the object of sex-morality is to save souls, hold to the more utilitarian view that its purpose is to safeguard the sanctity of the institution of marriage, are thus logically bound to regard the suppression of art and literature as serving the purpose of safeguarding private property.

I am not forgetting that marriage is frequently the result of falling in love. That aspect of it will be discussed in the next chapter. But love has nothing to do with the origin and development of the institution. So real is the economic nature of the institution of marriage that the modern emancipated woman, in spite of the confusion created in her mind by celebrating the transaction in a church instead of in a bank and by the stories of Adam and Eve and of Noah's Ark, cannot help regarding the economic aspect as paramount, even when she falls in love.

The modern emancipated woman is rebelling against the institution of patriarchal marriage, not for any such reasons as induced the primitive Christian Church to revolt against it, not because she objects to loving and being loved, or because she is not prepared to be faithful to one man, but because she objects to the economic arrangements. Whatever ignorance or deficiency in logic may be charged against her, she possesses the redeeming gift of realism. And when she is told by Professor Malinowski, or some other Adam-and-Eve anthropologist, that the family is the foundation of society, she is perfectly well able to see through the specious figure of speech, and to perceive that the term " family " is in this connection used as a euphemism for the man and his banking account, or whatever be the form of his private property, and that the plausible Adam-and-Eve sociological formula really means " Private property is the foundation of society." Under the economic arrangement of patriarchal marriage she neither possesses private property nor the means of acquiring any. She is therefore neither the foundation nor even a member of society. True that by selecting a husband with abundant private property she can have " all she wants," and is moreover spared all the bother of acquiring private property. But she retains a sufficient measure of the prejudices of traditional morality not to overlook the similarity between the arrangement and one which fastens an offensive name upon the woman who sells herself. Even if she is above such old-fashioned prejudices, people have a rooted objection to selling them-selves. She may, besides, be in love with her husband. And her realism enables her to perceive that the situation constitutes a profound danger to that love, and may even be fatal to it. The prejudice against selling herself has in this instance a more than superstitious value. That a man and a woman who love one another should agree to live together is an unnatural biological arrangement, as are most social arrangements, but it is culturally a very reasonable and desirable arrangement. Its reasonableness and desira-bility depend, however, entirely upon the circumstance that they do love one another, and if the arrangement is concluded in such a manner as to be prejudicial and even fatal to that love, it not only comes to savour of immorality and injustice, but becomes positively unpractical.

One of the many reasons why the arrangement is not conducive to the continuance of love is that the patriarchal husband, once the economic contract has been signed in the vestry or Register, and his own part of the bargain is duly fulfilled by providing for his wife's economic needs, considers naturally that her part of the bargain, namely, the dedication of her body, her love, her devotion, to himself and the complete dissolution of her personal interests into those of his private property—the foundation of society— should follow automatically as a matter of contracted duty. Love, in spite of formal rubrics which are not an essential part of the contract, is not his part of that contract; his part is economic, and having duly fulfilled it, he looks, according to all principles of business rectitude, to the due fulfilment of her part. If she fails to fulfil it with a good grace he will lament women's lack of the sense of business rectitude. If she alleges that she also requires love and devotion from him, he will lose patience at such displays of silly, hysterical feminine nonsense, and inform her that he has, like an honourable business man, faithfully fulfilled his part of the contract, and that the love and devotion business is her part, not his.

Instead of promoting the fulfilment of her part of the contract, patriarchal marriage rouses not only all the realism of modern emancipated woman, but throws her back upon unsophisticated biological dispositions. Those dispositions, stifled and overlayed by the cultural traditions of patriarchal society, surge up again in the intelligent modern woman. She tends to revert to the animal female who, very far from being urged to live in economic association with the male and to become part of the foundation of society, is impelled by all her biological reactions to regard the male as an enemy to whom she only yields herself masochistically at periodic intervals in order to become impregnated and to found her own version of the foundation of society, a family which has nothing whatever to do with him or his private property. Her attitude towards the male becomes self-defensive, and self-defence is the very reverse of love.

Patriarchal marriage is a masculine institution, and, in its sexual aspect, which is incidentally associated with its fundamental economic aspect, it is in accordance with masculine, not with feminine, sexual instincts. Those instincts, quite unlike those of the female, are fiercely dominating, subjugatory, masterful. The female is in the sight of the rutting male a prey over which his power as a conqueror and master has to be asserted. She is attacked, overpowered, bruised, mawled, wounded. Her injury, her resistance, her suffering, her subjugation are of the essence of crude, unsophisticated masculine sexual instincts. All this brutality, although it is the opposite of the female's masochistic instincts, is entirely acceptable to her. It is what her functional instincts expect of the male; it is the biological index of his eligibility as her impregnator. But it has nothing whatever to do with love, with his eligibility as a lifelong companion in an agreement for continued

cohabitation. Biological urges, in spite of all sentimentalizing Noah's Ark biology, are utterly unconcerned with that.

The revolt of modern emancipated woman against the
unfairness of patriarchal marriage leads her to revert to
biological values, to an attitude towards man which tends
more and more to partake of biological sex-antagonism, and
to eliminate the cultural developments which come under
the description of love.

XI

LOVE

Love is not a feature of the biological relation between the sexes. It is a cultural product. The statement may sound so strange to those whose minds are trained to the beautiful conception of Adam-and-Eve anthropology and Noah's Ark biology that they will find great difficulty in accepting it. The difficulty is all the greater because in order to understand the statement it is necessary to apprehend certain facts of natural history and social anthropology which are not emphasized in the current versions of those sciences.

The vocable "love" has been for ages employed as a synonymic appellation for the sexual urge. Synonyms come in particularly handy when the use of Anglo-Saxon words is liable to get one into trouble with the police. The more poetic the synonym the better. In Latin countries the sexual act is spoken of as "love." The same poetic circumlocution is in use in English-speaking countries. Animals are said in Noah's Ark natural histories to be engaged in love-making when they are mawling one another to death. The reproductive processes of vegetables are, by extension, commonly referred to as manifestations of love. The metaphor is even frequently extended to chemical affinities and to the force of universal gravitation, and love may be thus viewed as the ruling principle of the universe. A realistic contemplation of the universe is prone to arouse grave doubts as to that generalization.

The process of sexual copulation between a tiger and a tigress, or, for that matter, between a tom-cat and a tabby—which is more generally accessible to observation—is similarly liable to suggest doubts as to the identification of the sexual urge with love. The available information and observation concerning the operation of the sexual urges in uncultured humanity, in spite of the unsatisfactory character of reports from missionaries and rum-traders, is extremely emphatic and uniform in its testimony that what is commonly understood by love is not a marked trait in that quarter. Adam-and-Eve anthropologists have done their best to explain away that testimony, but it is too intractably unanimous to afford much scope for eclective methods. And there is a very clear and conclusive reason why love, as we understand it, should not be conspicuous in the sex relations of uncultured humanity. The manifestations of that sentiment are, in our own society, much more common and prominent in courtship than in marriage. In uncultured societies there is no courtship. That circumstance also explains why kissing is unknown in those societies. The kiss is a preliminary form of sexual approach. In uncultured societies there are no preliminaries.

It must not be imagined that savages are, as the unfortunate term suggests, brutal, bestial, and inhuman. Quite on the contrary, they are very agreeable and pleasant people. It is impossible for anyone to become acquainted with them and to live amongst them for some time without being drawn to them by feelings of affection. They are very nice people. And their niceness arises from their truly affectionate disposition. Indeed there is more love, in the general sense of the word, in uncultured than in cultured societies. There is a thousand times more love in a tribe of howling Melanesian cannibals than in any gathering of the fashionable in Mayfair or of the intellectuals in Chelsea. It is to that natural affectionate disposition, as I have repeatedly insisted, that human society owes the possibility of its rise out of animality—much more than to brain and cleverness. But the charming contrast between Melanesia and Mayfair, all to the advantage of the former, is due precisely to the fact that the affectionate disposition of the Melanesian savage is frittered away on all and sundry, whereas the men and women in Mayfair cordially detest one another and know perfectly well that they are themselves detested by most of their " friends." The latter state of things is very deplorable, but it is the inevitable result of a society founded upon individualism and the rights of private property—disguised at times, as we saw, as " the family." In such a society everyone, man or woman, must look after himself or herself first. Nobody else will. All the people with whom I have to deal are very nice people. They are really quite as affectionate in disposition as the Melanesian cannibals. I do firmly believe that when they rob me, cheat me, malign me, and kick me when I am down, they are grieved in their hearts at doing so. But *que voulez vous?* They must look after themselves first. They must also look after their families, their wives and children—the foundation of society. Consequently they cannot afford to waste much time in sympathy over the consequences of their having robbed, cheated, slandered, and kicked me. And each one of those people in Mayfair, or in Chelsea, or in the City knows that he is in exactly the same position in regard to everyone else. He cannot and does not expect much sympathy. He nor she.

And yet, despite everything, they are essentially affectionate people. They are just as affectionate as the Melanesian cannibal. Human nature has not changed in that respect. If anything it has improved. The modern men and women are probably more tenderly and deeply affectionate than the cannibals. They show it in the infallible appeal of sentiment, of sentimentality, however sugary and soppy, which they can indulge in without jeopardizing their own safety. They feel their position. It is simply intolerable, heart-racking. Their situation in a universe of love is insufferable. Each of them, man or woman, longs, if the truth be told, for sympathy and affection. Each longs beyond anything in the world to be able to put aside, if only for a short interval of respite, his or her self-defensive armour, the terrible necessity of looking after themselves, of being on their guard, of distrusting every other human being. They long for love.

The Melanesian cannibal doesn't. He has no need for it. The experience of the Mayfair and Chelsea and City people of having to be watchfully on their guard every minute of their lives against their friends is unknown in Melanesia. The Melanesian knows indeed that were he to wander into the next tribe, he must look out for himself. The next tribe are strangers, they are what he calls enemies. He is quite prepared to show no mercy and to expect none so far as they are concerned. But he does not live among strangers as every Mayfair or Chelsea man or woman does. He lives among friends. They have never sought to rob him, or cheat him, or slander him. If he is down, if he has had bad luck, if he has nothing to eat, they will vie with one another in supplying him with food. They will make a point of going hungry themselves rather than he should. And they will not even make a virtue of it, and think how very noble they are and how grateful he should be. Nay, if he has no wife, some one of his friends will press him to have a loan of his own. " That's going a bit too far," say our righteous moralists. Let them cast the beam out of their own eye before they have the effrontery to talk about morals and the foundations of society. According to the foundations of the Melanesian's society he knows not what it is to be surrounded by people not one of whom he can trust should he have need of help, but who are constantly discoursing about morals. Consequently he knows not love in the sense of a society where it means a partial respite and release from that intolerable position. His sexual urges are brutal and fierce enough, as they are with all natural males. He is not particularly unkind towards his sexual associates, but he is no kinder towards them than towards any other person. He makes it a rule to obtain them from some other tribelet or group. Perhaps the desire that his masculine sexual urges shall not be hampered by too much tenderness and soft-hearted sympathy may have something to do with that strict rule of his. He asks for no love from his mate. Why should he? He is not love-starved. He does not understand what you mean when you ask whether he loves his wife and whether she loves him. She, as a matter of fact, very often does, because he is a very decent fellow, loyal to his friends to the point of Quixotism, and thoroughly able to deal with his enemies. And she admires him, as he well deserves.

But the poor wretched Mayfairite is not so fortunately situated as the Melanesian cannibal. He is by nature just as decent and affectionate. But his unfortunate situation in a highly civilized society professing a religion of love and moral traditions causes him to eat his heart out for want of common human affection. That affectionate disposition which was the very foundation of human society in the savage state is, in fact, one of the ruling passions of civilized man. And no wonder. Civilization has starved it to the point of despair. It is a psychological law that ruling passions tend to fuse. Another ruling passion of moral civilized man is that which rules all life, animal and human, the urge of sex. The two ruling passions, the longing for trustful affection and the passion of sex become fused in civilized man.

They are entirely different. They have nothing to do with one another. They are even radically opposite. Yet being both ruling passions, both repressed and starved, both desperately seeking an outlet, they have become fused. The affection which is in the savage associated with social relations is in civilized man concentrated on sex relations. When the wretched civilized man, even the most hardened and cynical, reads in the eyes of a woman whom he desires that he need not be on his guard with her, that he can trust her, that she loves him, the natural affectionate disposition of his nature wells up from him.

The look in the woman's eyes recalls to him his mother, almost the only human being whom he could trust, who, he knew, would not betray him and endeavour to get the better of him. He is overcome with tenderness. That tenderness has nothing whatever to do with his masculine desire for the woman's body. It blends with that desire. The breaking-down of the barriers of sex-tabus and sex-segregation is identified with the breaking-down of the barriers of compulsive self-defensive mistrust, of individual segregation. And the promise of release from the latter constitutes the most potent sexual attraction.

But the two things have biologically nothing in common. So distinct are they that even traditional values regard them as opposed. The one is accounted noble, the other base, the one pure, the other impure. For once traditional evaluations correspond, in their contrast at least, to the facts of life. And even to some extent to its values. Human values can have no other meaning than their relation to the facts of human social life. Love being in its origin the very spring of that social life, is, if anything is, good and noble. That lust is therefore base does not follow. But it is, at any rate, the psychological opposite of love. Every expert in matters erotic knows that tenderness, affection, and even respect are sentiments opposed to the full biological operation of the predatory and pugnacious masculine sexual urges. Their fulfilment requires, in whatever measure, a reversion to the brutal, dominating attitude of the animal male. It requires in some degree the elimination of love. The perfect purity of Puritan and Christian theory would be biologically equivalent to sterilization. To look upon every woman as a sister would obviously be equivalent to race-suicide. All visionary doctrines of purity as an absolute value, unless they go to their logical term in accepting race-suicide, postulate the necessity of impurity. The biological urges see to it that such visionary doctrines are never carried out in practice. Platonic love is notoriously precarious. Affection between the sexes is inevitably associated with the sexual urge. But the converse does not hold : the sexual urge can quite well dispense with affection.

The peculiar association of love with sex brought about by social individualism—the latter is itself no less an incongruity, individualism being the direct opposite of socialism—is an inexhaustible source of confusions, dilemmas, and irreducible incongruities.

One of those incongruities is the old dilemma of the patriarchal male between the ideal of womanly virtue conforming to patriarchal requirements and his biological urges. That dilemma was, as is well known, solved by the ancient Greeks by subdividing womankind into two sharply distinct classes, and by having both virtuous wives and accomplished, natural, and unvirtuous companions. It has been solved down to our time in a similiar manner by supplementing patriarchal marriage with prostitution. But while the Greek companion was accomplished and honoured, the Christian prostitute is a miserable and debased thing which inspires a pity more incompatible with sexual fulfilment than the most accomplished pattern of patriarchal virtue. The Christian prostitute is as wretched a failure as the Christian wife. Christianity has accordingly

given an enormous impetus to adultery and fornication
which were all but unknown in pagan Greece. The old Greek
cited by Athenæus who remarked that feminine purity
and virtue, offering as they do more scope to being outraged, are an additional stimulus to masculine gratification,
was an exception. This outraging of wives is a fertile source
of trouble in patriarchal marriage. The wife who conforms
in all points to the patriarchal ideal of what she should be
resents being outraged, or treated, as she puts it, as if she
were a prostitute. That she should be treated so is in her
eyes proof conclusive that she is neither loved nor
respected. The patriarchal marriage is thus wrecked by
the ideally patriarchal perfection of the wife. Husbands
with an ounce of prudence will accordingly refrain from
outraging their wives, and, their natural masculine urges
being frustrated, will supplement patriarchal marriage
by squalid prostitution or adultery. The ideal patriarchal
wife belongs, of course, to the Days of Ignorance rather
than to the present age, but post-Puritanical values, though
reinterpreted, are apt to survive under the specious guise
of the real opposition between love and lust. The
outrageous character of masculine sexual urges are
accounted by the noble and affectionate wife incompatible
with love, and to be treated as a prostitute, instead of
being regarded by her as the clinching confirmation of
sexual comradeship, is looked upon as an intolerable insult.
The old situation repeats itself. The husband is liable
to succumb to the attraction of the woman who " understands him so much better." Quite commonly, of course,
the situation is reversed. The intelligent woman loses all

patience with the post-Puritanical husband who could not
think of treating her as a prostitute. The conflict of
irreconcilable values, which is of the essence of morbid
sexuality in the individual, is reproduced in the morbidity
of marriage.

That love, more particularly in the male, does not
survive sexual possession is a current commonplace. The
truth which has given the commonplace its currency is,
of course, the fact that biological urges are nowise adapted
to the continued cohabitation of marriage. Those of the
male are adapted to their biological function of wide
dissemination; those of the female to segregation from the
male as soon as she becomes impregnated. Even to the
highly civilized female the male becomes utterly repellent
from that time until her offspring has become independent
of her care. But the commonplace assumes the misconception that love is equivalent to the sexual urges, whereas
it is merely adventitiously associated with them. The
truth or falsehood of the current commonplace will depend
in any particular case on the extent in which the motive
of sexual association is biological attraction or love. The
former is not a possible foundation of continued association. And, on the other hand, if it be absent or precarious,
love is not a sexual association. Thus the biologically
unnatural association depends upon the permutations and
combinations of countless factors.

That unnatural association of man and woman
constitutes for cultured humanity the most complete
fulfilment of human relations. But, far from being an
automatically established social product as Adam-and-Eve

anthropology suggests, it is a superlatively artificial cultural ideal. Like all ideals it is extremely difficult of fulfilment. Its fulfilment depends not only upon very complex combinations and permutations, but, above all, upon very considerable understanding of facts and intelligence. Those difficult conditions are in every possible manner impeded by every current theory and assumption bearing on the subject, and their fulfilment is carefully and ingeniously prevented by every measure taken to safeguard the sanctity of patriarchal marriage.

XII

MARRIAGE-LAW ATROCITIES

I SOUGHT to point out that superstitious tabus, supposing their provisions to be highly desirable, are nevertheless profoundly objectionable in principle and effect because superstitious tabus are not enforced with a view to desirable provisions, but superstitiously, fanatically, and tyrannically. I make no apology for repeating the remark, for it appears difficult to apprehend. Only the other day I endeavoured to make it clear to an audience of distinguished anthropologists. After I had spoken for an hour on that point, several distinguished anthropologists took the trouble to point out that " after all," some tabus have beneficial effects. I was overwhelmed with the sense of my incapacity for logical expression.

What I so inadequately sought to point out concerning alleged beneficial tabus applies similarly, but in a far higher degree, to the institution of marriage as it exists to-day in Western culture. " In a far higher degree," because the alleged beneficial effects of superstitious tabus are in every instance very disputable, whereas the reasonableness of the principle of monogamic marriage is unquestionable. In the present state of civilization the arrangement that two persons, a man and a woman, who are deeply attached to each other should live together and make common cause in their interests is the most reasonable and satisfactory arrangement that can be devised. I can think of no improvement upon it. But—as with our

162

hypothetical beneficial tabus—when that reasonable and satisfactory arrangement is enforced, not on account of its reasonableness or satisfactory character, but as a sacrosanct moral institution, that is, superstitiously, fanatically, and tyrannically, it is at once transformed into a detestable, revolting, and intolerable iniquity.

It is reasonable and satisfactory for a man and a woman to agree to the arrangement for which monogamic marriage stands. For the sake of convenience in carrying out the administrative duties in a civilized country it is not unreasonable that they should give notice of the arrangement to the clerk who keeps statistical records. So far everything is unobjectionable. But if they are in any way penalized should they fail to be so obliging as to furnish the information to the clerk, they may very justly raise the question what his statistical records have to do with their agreement. And should they find that the omission to oblige the clerk with the information, instead of rendering them liable to a fine of, say, two shillings and sixpence for failing to assist him in keeping his statistics, renders them liable to be completely ostracized by their friends, insulted by hotel-keepers and passport officials, and generally treated as pariahs, they may begin to wonder what is the meaning of that reasonable and satisfactory institution.

Our happy couple will, in answer to their natural inquiries, be referred to the Bible and to other ancient religious documents; they will be told that they are not " really married "; that they are living in a state of sin; and that the reasonable and satisfactory arrangement which they have made is not monogamic marriage at all, but free love. Free love and free thought are understood in democratic Western cultures founded on hard-won freedom to be terms of severe moral reprobation. The reasonable institution of marriage is understood in Western culture to be founded upon love and upon the freedom of choice of the parties concerned. A marriage which is not the outcome of love is accounted immoral, and one which is not the outcome of the free choice of both parties is accounted impermissible. But although marriage is avowedly founded on love and freedom, free love is nevertheless accounted the opposite of marriage.

The difference between the two depends neither on love nor on freedom, but on whether notice of the arrangement has, or has not, been given to the clerk in charge of statistics. It turns out that the notice to the clerk is not regarded in the light of statistical information obligingly supplied by the happy couple to the authorities, but that it is held to constitute the marriage. In fact, the couple are not married by their love or by their mutual agreement, but by the clerk. The languages of Western culture preserve in a fossilized form the archæological survival of social conditions in which marriage had no reference whatever to love, and the freedom of choice of the parties had nothing to do with it, but the institution was an economic arrangement contracted by the tribe, the clans concerned, and not by the man and the woman concerned. The curious savage notion which is embodied in fossil form in our languages still survives in Timbuctoo and among the wilder tribes of Australian savages. We accordingly speak

of " getting married " as a passive verbal expression of
which the active subject is not the man or the woman, but
the clerk, priest, or other person who " marries " them.
People do not marry one another, but require some third
person to " marry " them. The savage linguistic survival
still causes some grammatical confusion, as when a servant-
girl asks the vicar to marry her, or a man speaks of
marrying his daughter.

Not only is the entry made in his records by the clerk
held to supplant the agreement made by the man and the
woman, but by a sort of forgery the clerk falsifies that
agreement and substitutes for it an entirely different one.
He introduces a clause which renders it indissoluble. Like
simple persons, such as an inexperienced author who falls
into the hands of an unscrupulous publisher and carelessly
signs an outrageous agreement without first consulting his
lawyer, the enamoured couple are too unwary to pay much
attention to that sharp practice. In the romantic language
of their emotional state they not only declare their affection
for each other, but do not hesitate to swear that it can
never change. They should, of course, consult a lawyer
before signing any rash legal document, and he should
protect them against the Register clerk's sharp practice
when the latter unscrupulously takes advantage of their
emotional state. But the law, instead of protecting them,
conspires in the mean fraud practised upon them. It offers
them every inducement and facility to sign the agreement
in the greatest hurry while they are under the influence of
their emotional condition, and only charges them a few
shillings for the clerk's trouble. But once the fraud has

been successfully perpetrated upon them, the entire force of the law is mobilized to enforce rigorously its consequences. The love which was supposed to be the indispensable condition of the arrangement may entirely disappear and turn to utter hatred. The freedom of choice which was considered essential to rendering the arrangement valid may emphatically demand its termination. But that freedom of choice can no longer, in virtue of the entry made by the clerk, be exercised. The arrangement founded upon love and freedom of choice must be carried out under conditions of antagonism and coercion. The change from an emotional state of love to one of antagonism may by no means be due to the mere transiency and fickleness of human emotions. The inexperienced enamoured couple, who have been surreptitiously, hastily, and fraudulently married by the Register clerk, may discover at once that they have committed a ghastly mistake. The young wife may discover that she has been the victim of a cruel fraud, not only on the part of the clerk, but also on the part of her husband. He may be an utter scoundrel, he may be a drunkard, a criminal, he may be diseased in body or in mind. He may quite commonly be such a fool or such a cad that to compel any woman to live with him continuously is the most cruel form of torture that can be inflicted upon her. Or things may be the other way; the man may discover that he has taken unto himself a fiend in human form. Those conditions which, in varying degrees, constitute the deepest form of complete ruin which human lives can suffer, are only definable in the vaguest terms. Their legal description is covered by the colourless word

" incompatibility," which may mean anything from the irritation of two people who have nothing in common to an inferno the very contemplation of which fills one with horror.

It is customary to remark : " So vital an association as that between man and woman should not be hastily, lightly, and rashly dissolved. A passing quarrel, a transient mood may sever a relation which, but for such a fleeting cloud, may be the fullest realization of lifelong happiness. All lovers quarrel. Human happiness should not be jeopardized by momentary impulses. All association demands patience, forbearance, and the adaptation that can only come from the prolonged practice of that toleration." The remark is profoundly wise advice. But, once more, there is a whole world of difference between wise advice and coercion. The clerk who registers the intimate private agreement between two persons in an emotional state is empowered to coerce them into continuing that agreement in whatsoever circumstances so long as they live.

The fantastic tyranny of that insane power is so monstrous that civilized countries like England have been compelled to make provisions for divorce. They have only done so within the last hundred years. They have done so after the fiercest and most persistent resistance; they have done so with the utmost reluctance; they have done so to the smallest extent compatible with appeasing the exasperation of indignant victims. They have done so in the most objectionable manner possible. " Getting married " is quite easy. Every facility is offered to enamoured couples for obtaining the services of a clerk to " marry " them. The expense is negligible. The formality is reduced to a minimum. But should the gravest and most urgent reasons occur for dissolving the association, such as the protection of the woman from a murderous or drunken husband, or the latter's confinement in a lunatic asylum or in jail, the most elaborate, solemn, and ponderous legal machinery must be laboriously set in motion. The clerk who had power to " marry " the couple has no power in this instance. The woman must first consult a lawyer, who will for a consideration be good enough to take a languid interest in her tragic case. After he has knit his brows, pondering over the difficult problem, after he has with unhasting industry accumulated sheaves of stamped paper, the problem is humbly submitted to the judgment of a court, with gown and periwig complete, solemnly assembled as for the trial of a murder, and after a full discussion of every detail of the humble petitioner's married life, the learned judge may, with much display of moral reluctance and with a full sense of the boldness and gravity of his act, see his way to granting a hesitant and conditional decree *nisi*, to be made absolute, if after mature consideration there appears to be no reason to repent of the rash liberality, in six months' time. The expenses incurred to obtain this oracle of the wigged and gowned gentlemen are appalling. The woman will be fortunate if she obtains her freedom at the price of a hundred pounds or so.

This in the gravest and most desperate cases of marriage. In ordinary and commonplace cases of the misfortune, such as the total wreck of a woman's or a man's life by cohabitation with an absolutely impossible associate, the procedure is exactly the same. Total wreck of one or two lives is not, however, in English law a sufficient ground for divorce. According to existing English law, in order to obtain release from the coercive association imposed by the clerk at the Register Office, the man or the woman is required to " commit adultery." Needless to say, such being the monstrous character of the English institution of marriage, the great majority of people take the law more or less into their own hands. The " facilities " offered for relief from the institution are only taken advantage of when it is absolutely impossible to do otherwise. The parties who are not permitted to enter into free association, resort to free separation. They are, however, prevented from marrying again. It is this remarrying which is technically known as " committing adultery," and which renders resort to the mercy of the law indispensable. As is natural, after a more or less prolonged and complete separation, the wife or the husband meets a man or woman with whom the chance of proving the desirability and reasonableness of the institution of marriage appears to be better than in the first experiment. In order to give that desirable and reasonable institution another chance a divorce must be obtained. The young woman, say, after much heart-searching and with the benefit of the experience and wisdom which she was legally supposed to lack entirely when she contracted the first association, has discovered that, in spite of that disastrous experience, monogamic marriage is quite possible, reasonable, and desirable. She requires to be relieved from the intolerable and atrocious penalties to which she is subjected on account of her favourable and conservative views on the institution. She cannot obtain that relief without the assistance and co-operation of her first husband. Unless the latter is a particularly contemptible and vindictive blackguard, he will assist her by " giving her her freedom." Should it, however, transpire in the course of eventual proceedings that he is not an utter blackguard, the court will, with all the solemnity and moral dignity for which English law is universally admired, arraign him for not being a blackguard. The crime of which he is guilty, and which consists in being in complete agreement with his former wife as to the desirability of separating, is technically known as " collusion," and is described as a form of contempt of court and as an attempt to defraud justice. The court, in all such cases, employs its shrewdness and acumen chiefly in guarding against such a scandalous offence, and in scenting out any indication that the dissolution of the marriage is equally desired by all parties concerned. Should any indication of that outrageous state of affairs appear, the proceedings are stopped, and the indignation of the mouthpiece of the law soars to heights of true eloquence in the expression of moral indignation. In the interests of literature and of the deservedly high repute of British oratory, it is earnestly to be hoped that a collection of those speeches will some day be made and published for the instruction and edification of posterity. The slightest indication of " collusion," such as a formal exchange of letters, abolishes any possibility of the young wife being liberated. She must by order of the court continue to commit "adultery." Only if her former husband's petition can be shown to proceed from purely vindictive motives, can it be considered. "Adultery" must be proved. In the great majority of cases the "adulteress" is not at all a woman of light sexual conduct, nor has she indulged in impulsive "misconduct." She is probably the most conventionally pure, chaste, and moral person in the court. She must submit to having her whole sexual life discussed in detail. The evidence of detectives, servants, hotel managers, waiters, is called in. The state of her bedroom is described. She is publicly insulted by periwigged persons who, properly speaking, are in most cases not morally worthy of kissing her shoes.

The sinister grotesqueness embodied in the English law of marriage can only be touched upon. It would require a volume to explore the maze of its grim imbecility. While, for instance, the petitioning husband must be proved to be moved solely by the vindictive motives of a cad, and he must not only cause his wife to commit adultery, but is entitled to be paid for doing so, should he likewise have committed adultery the indissolubility of his marriage is thereby secured. The Gilbertian theory is that he can apply for a dissolution of the marriage only if he does so in the character of an offended party. In point of fact, of course, in more than ninety per cent. of the cases in which a husband petitions for divorce on the ground of his wife's adultery, he alone is the guilty party in so far as there can be any question of guilt in the matter. The woman, who in legal obscene jargon is termed an "adulteress,"

is in the great majority of cases a very much injured lady
whom a brutal, or idiotically foolish and neglectful, or
otherwise intolerable husband has in the first place driven
away from her home, and who has further been driven
to the verge of distraction by being compelled by the law
to " commit adultery." Not only does the law compel her
to commit adultery, and to supply detailed evidence of the
manner of her doing so, and thereafter subject her for
doing so to insults intolerable to a refined woman, but
after having submitted to the humiliation of those insults
for the sake of obtaining her freedom, she is further
permanently subjected to the like insults on the part of
society in general. As I write, the day's newspaper contains the Lord Chamberlain's public announcement that
the wife of an officer who has highly distinguished himself
in the King's service is forbidden to appear at Court,
the reason being that she had been divorced by her first
husband. No person to whom an English court of law has
granted a divorce is permitted to approach the throne of
Henry VIII.

Such is the sacrosanct institution of marriage in England,
to safeguard which is the professed purpose of morals.
Puritan America is in this respect not quite so fantastically
barbaric as Puritan England. The comparative facility, still
far too complex, costly, and vexatious, with which the
registration of a marriage can be rescinded in some
American States is an inexhaustible theme for the jeers
and the moral indignation of righteous England.

Future civilized generations will, there can be no doubt,
view the moral marriage laws of England with the same

horror and detestation with which present generations look back upon the juridic torture, the disembowellings and quarterings of sixteenth-century moral laws. English matrimonial legislation inflicts suffering much more widespread and subtly cruel than any Star Chamber or Spanish Inquisition ever did. More women are persecuted to-day as wives than two hundred years ago as witches. The reasonable and desirable institution of monogamic marriage constitutes in England to-day an atrocity, an infamy so vile and execrable that men and women with a modicum of intelligence and of moral self-respect ought, on principle, to decline to oblige the clerk of civic statistics with the notification of their personal and private arrangements. Had they any moral courage they would face persecution rather than countenance a lewd and nauseating hypocritical tyranny which appertains to barbarism and not to civilization.

I am as familiar with the current apologetic formulas adduced in excuse of English matrimonial juridic atrocities as with those adduced in excuse of sixteenth-century executions for treason or in excuse of the Holy Inquisition. Everyone is familiar with them. Almost everyone is also aware of their speciousness and invalidity. The safety of the English throne in the sixteenth century did not require that persons suspected of disloyal views should be publicly castrated and that their bellies should be ripped open at the Marble Arch. The excuse was not adequate. The English courts of justice which passed that sentence were savage institutions. Neither the discouraging of hasty and impulsive separations, nor the pseudo-problems raised in regard to children or to property constitute adequate excuses for the savage institution of English divorce courts. Children are not generally nowadays brought up in homes, and the sooner children who are brought up in homes held together by the dread of the divorce court are relieved from that handicap, the better for them and for all concerned.

Why is it that the perfectly reasonable and highly desirable arrangement that a man and a woman should live together in lifelong association turns out to be, as carried out in England, an infamous and barbaric institution? We are brought back for the answer to our starting-point, the subtle distinction which professors of anthropology are not equal to apprehending, namely, that the effects of a rational arrangement carried out on superstitious grounds are not beneficial, but baneful. The institution of monogamic marriage does not rest, in England, upon the reasonable and desirable grounds for the arrangement. It rests upon the Christian superstition that fornication is to be put down. It rests upon the barbaric conception that a woman acquired in marriage by a legal transaction is personal property. The institution is not enforced as a reasonable and desirable arrangement, but superstitiously, fanatically, and tyrannically. As with superstitious tabus, it is not any beneficial effects which those tabus may produce which is the motive for enforcing them, but the superstitions to which they owe their origin. Reasonable motives give rise to reasonable institutions; superstitious motives which are survivals of savagery give rise to savage institutions.

XIII

SEX JUSTICE

THE grotesque incongruity which, in the current usage of Western culture, assigns the appellation of " morality " to sexual restrictions exclusively, ignoring as appertaining to a lower plane of ethical obligations, justice, intellectual and social honesty, charity, and every moral demand on the conduct of human beings in their social relations, is not only grotesque, but grossly immoral. It is doubtless owing, in part at least, to that inherent immorality of Western conceptions that the appreciation of the claims of justice is so poorly developed. The moral sense of Western culture, while it watches with sleuth-like vigilance on so-called public morals, that is, on the use of tabu words in printed literature or on representations or exhibitions of the human body, is entirely torpid and callous where the gross abuses and flagrant injustices of its social order are concerned. Western morality is quick at suppressing literature, but slow at suppressing war; zealous in the abolition of obscene postcards, but lukewarm in the abolition of obscene slums; active in putting down white slavery, but apathetic in putting down wage slavery; alert in preventing vice, but slothful in putting down starvation; shocked at clothing insufficient for purposes of modesty, but indifferent to clothing insufficient for purposes of warmth. It spares no effort to secure a perfectly pure world, but is ready to tolerate a perfectly iniquitous one. Its efforts are wholly successful in eliminating indecency, but wholly unsuccessful in eliminating injustice. The " morality " of Western culture is a scandal.

That profoundly immoral tradition is mainly responsible for the chaos of uncertainty attendant upon the decay of the authority of sexual tabus. Many men and women having discovered that those tabus are superstitions destitute of moral grounds or of reasonable motive, draw the conclusion that there is no sexual morality. That conclusion does not, of course, follow, and is as absurd as the tabus. The relations between the sexes are, like all other human social relations, subject to moral principles without which social existence would be impossible. Being much more complex, fundamental, and close than any other human relation, they call for the application of those principles in an even higher degree.

The principles of social morality are not obscure, mystical, or doubtful. Only inspired teachers, profound philosophers, pedantic professors, and learned legislators have succeeded in reducing morality to a fog of perplexity. The principles of social morality are so simple as to be understood and taken as a matter of course by the rudest savages. They are comprised in one word : justice. Right is the opposite of wrong; and wrong consists in inflicting injuries on other people. It has taken two thousand years of Christian morality to obscure the moral conscience of mankind. Morality derives its authority from the natural operation of social relations between human beings. People resent being injured. They therefore regard those who injure them as wrongdoers. The natural objection of human individuals to being injured by others is the foundation of morality, and has, on the whole, promoted the steady advance of justice in civilized societies. Every advance in the application of the principles of justice, that is, every advance in morality, has been the result of the strong objection of people to being injured by others. The automatic operation of that cause affords solid ground for the hope that human society will, in spite of immoral traditions and their zealous defence by interested persons, continue to become more moral, and that the scandalous distortion of moral standards by Christianity is, like other injustices, bound eventually to disappear.

To the great credit of human nature most people are restrained in their sexual conduct, not so much by considerations of tabu-morality as by considerations of justice and kindness. Infringements of traditional sexual restrictions, however unreasonable those restrictions may be, are under existing conditions a cause of great injury and suffering. The majority of men, even though they may not be impressed by the authority of moral tabus, are strongly influenced by their reluctance to inflict injury and suffering. The hesitation of Faust on the threshold of Gretchen's cottage did not arise from an innate reverence for the tabu of chastity, but from the innate sensitiveness of social man as regards the infliction of an injury upon an innocent person. But the gross injuries to innocent persons which result from unchastity are not the direct effect of that unchastity, but of social tabus on unchastity. They are not the effects of immorality, but of traditional morality. They are penalties inflicted by a ferociously

M

moral world for breaches of its superstitious savage tabus.

Christian society, accordingly, with a logic corresponding to its morality, vents its vengeance upon the victim rather than upon the author of the injury. In Mexico, I am told, it is dangerous to invoke the aid of the police should you happen to have your pocket picked. You run a good chance of being clapped into jail until the matter has been cleared up. Christian morality proceeds on much the same principles as the Mexican police. The cad does not incur a much more severe penalty at the hands of our moral police than that of being regarded as a gay dog. The girl is quite literally ruined. She is all the more thoroughly ruined in proportion as the instilled principles of her morality conform to Christian ideals. If they do not, if she happens to be sufficiently emancipated from those principles to face her persecutors boldly and brazenly, the moral Christian or pseudo-Christian world behaves in the same manner as do vicious curs when they find that you are not frightened at them. It slinks away and leaves off barking.

Apart from the untold injustices and atrocities inflicted by moral tradition for breaches of its superstitious tabus, which constitute by far the larger proportion of the sufferings consequent upon unchastity, inconsiderate unchastity may result in injustice. In the great majority of uncultured societies unmarried girls are free to be as unchaste as they please without suffering any social penalties or condemnation. But in most of those societies the converse aspect of that recognized freedom is also rigorously observed. Rape is regarded as an intolerable offence. A young woman whose right to give herself is recognized has also the right to refuse herself.

Rape is not a common offence in civilized societies. The term " seduction," with its patriarchal implications of feminine mental helplessness and passivity, has practically dropped out of use in modern speech. The discarding of the term is not altogether justified. It is as possible to be dishonest in love as in business. To obtain sexual gratification by false pretences is as common as to obtain money by the same means. The current toleration of fraud in business transactions does not altogether excuse its employment in sex relations. To induce by false pretences a woman to yield herself is unjust and immoral. It is, of course, every bit as unjust and immoral for a woman to seduce a man by false pretences as for a man to seduce a woman. A man who deliberately deceives a woman as to the nature of the relation between them is a cad. A woman who deliberately deceives a man as to the nature of those relations is likewise a cad. Allowance has to be made for the delusions of erotic emotion sedulously fostered by sentimentalizing moral tradition. But there is, over and above that involuntary self-deception, far more insincerity and fraud in the relations between the sexes than there should be. That fraud is itself largely the outcome of the same tradition. It assumes that all " courtship " is a form of seductive persuasion, and that every woman requires, consistently with the character of her patriarchal " virtue," to be persuaded, that is to say, seduced. The woman who can give herself without being

seduced is condemned by patriarchal Christian tradition
as being of " easy virtue." Patriarchal Christian morality
thus sanctifies seduction. It indulgently recognizes the
fraud which it accounts necessary to overcome the
" virtue " of a woman by such principles as " All is fair
in love and war." There is, on the contrary, no relation
in which honesty and honour are more indispensable than
in the love-relation. Mutual trust, which is what love in the
deepest psychological significance of the term really means,
is of the essence of that relation. Every breach of that
mutual trust saps the foundation of that relation which
consists of psychological no less than of physical intimacy.
It converts sexual association into sexual antagonism.

The worst form of heartless seduction is, of course,
marriage. Every woman who goes through the marriage
service is being seduced in aggravated circumstances with
the complicity and assistance of the officiating priest. The
clergymen who act as accessories to those frauds are
deceivers of the blackest dye. The conscience of every
clergyman ought to give him no peace on account of the
women he has ruined.

Christian and Puritan moral tradition prescribes the
maximum amount of dishonesty in the relation between
the sexes and in every sentiment arising out of it. The
difficulties, the antagonisms, the conflicts which beset that
relation are mainly the outcome of that prescriptive riot of
dishonesty. Nothing would contribute more towards their
solution and the dissipation of the conflicts of individual
interests than the substitution of a little realistic honesty
for Christian fraudulence. What is immoral in the

relations between the sexes, and therefore apt to cause inevitable injury, is mendacity, pretence, and hypocrisy, all, that is to say, that is enjoined, commended, and enforced by a pretentious, mendacious and hypocritical system of morality. No standards of conduct, no legislative enactments, no revolution of opinion as regards social norms can be of any real effect in bringing about harmony in the relation between the sexes so long as those relations continue to be prescriptively suffused with false pretence, mendacity, and hypocrisy.

Sex relations which are founded upon crude economic or commercial considerations, sexual relations which are founded on physical appetence alone may be perfectly just and honest. There is as a rule no more just and honest dealing in sex relations than that of the prostitute. The immorality of prostitution does not lie in the prostitute's behaviour, but in the social immorality which compels her to have recourse to her branch of commerce. Whether that branch of commerce is for a woman a desirable one is a matter of intelligence and taste. In ancient Greece women of the highest intelligence and taste adopted from choice the mode of life of *hetairai*, which was not quite equivalent to prostitution, and was in many respects preferable to the severe purdah imposed upon Greek wives. The commercial prostitution which has flourished in Christian Europe, but with the decay of Christian morality is tending to become obsolete, does not appeal to women of intelligence and good taste. The reason is that it does not provide sufficient sexual freedom. A woman of intelligence and cultivated taste aspires to be free to fulfil more adequately the possibilities of happiness which sex offers. For exactly similar reasons she will abstain from promiscuity. And the greater her intelligence and cultured appreciation of the possibilities of sexual happiness, the greater will be her restraint in this respect.

In a passage already quoted,[1] Dean Inge makes the interesting admission that the Christian virtue of chastity is not founded on justice, that is, on our duty to others. It is founded, he informs us, on duty to ourselves. That sounds like a contradiction in terms. Duty is what we owe to others; what we owe to ourselves entails a special method of book-keeping. As I pointed out, both our duty to others and the observance of tabus invested with extra-rational sanctity, may be regarded as duties which we owe to ourselves. A Jew owes to his self-respect to abstain from eating pork, a Hindu to abstain from eating cow-flesh. But chastity may quite well be a duty to others, and it is, in fact, as such, and not as a duty to ourselves, that it has become enforced as a social virtue. Chastity, apart from its special ritual and magic uses, has commonly been enforced as a duty which women owed to men. The Jesuit missionaries in China were much troubled by the discovery that the Christian conception of chastity was gross and rudimentary by comparison with the exalted notions of the Chinese. In the matter of purity the Chinese women could give points to the most sexophobic Christian Fathers. But the weak side of Chinese morality was that the virtue was entirely confined in its scope to women. The fastidiousness of Chinese women's virtue was

[1] See above, p. 77.

such that it offered insuperable obstacles to the ministra-
tions of the Padres, and rendered it impossible for them
to administer the sacraments to female converts or hear
their confessions. But when the Padres sought to talk
the matter over with the ladies' male relatives, or with
grave and influential mandarins, they were received in
apartments adorned with the most ingeniously obscene
pornographic pictures, and their hosts offered, as a matter
of ordinary civility, to entertain them with sexual orgies.
When the Fathers spoke to the men of the duty of
chastity, the Chinese no more understood what they
meant than if they had spoken of the duty of men to
suckle babies.

The Chinese women, thoroughly imbued with patriarchal
principles and persuaded that their sole function in life
was to please the men, regarded chastity as very much a
duty to others. And it is, in fact, emphatically as a duty
to others that, in Christian countries, chastity is regarded
as incumbent upon women, while the duty is looked upon
as weighing much more lightly upon men. Chastity may,
in truth, be a very clear duty to others imposed by common
principles of elementary justice and honesty. If a man and
a woman promise, expect, and understand that mutual
fidelity shall be observed by them, a breach of that fidelity
is unjust and dishonest. The restriction imposed upon their
sexual freedom is a matter of common social justice and
honesty.

The emancipated and intelligent modern woman rightly
regards Chinese morality as an outrageous piece of andro-
cratic tyranny. That does not prevent her from being quite

willing to be faithful to a man whose affection she values and who expects fidelity of her. If she is not, she is not only unjust and dishonest, but unintelligent. For, like the commercial prostitute, she sets aside her opportunity of deriving from her sex the measure of happiness which it can afford.

That measure of happiness is largely a matter of cultivated taste. Cultivated civilized taste has considerably enriched the relations between the sexes. The intelligent civilized woman who understands her own value and the value to her of her *couturière* and beauty specialist, would be very much distressed if her powers of sexual attraction did not exceed those of a black and malodorous savage woman from Central Australia. So would the civilized male. The intelligent civilized woman may indignantly repudiate the Chinese maxim that the sole function of women is to afford pleasure to men. But she, at the same time, is anything but indifferent to her powers of sexual attraction. In attaching some importance to these, she is not manifesting mere vanity or biological femininity, but intelligence. For she knows that she is thereby increasing the possible happiness to be derived from her sexual disposition. And in the same manner as sex-appeal is not quite the same thing in Central Australia as in London, so it varies considerably in different cultural environments. It was entirely different in Victorian England from what it is among intelligent men and women at the present day. The prescriptive masculine sentiment of Victorian romance had in view the chaste devotion of the flower-like and demure Victorian young lady with convoluted skirts and an unconvoluted brain, whose mind held out the promise of maturing into the placid stupor of respectable futility while her pure body matured into housewifely adiposity. That ideal Victorian young lady would stand, at the present day, a very good chance of preserving her unsullied purity for the term of her natural life. At a still earlier period the eighteenth-century French or Italian young lady who had undergone a perfect upbringing in a convent and fulfilled every patriarchal ideal until after the honeymoon, became after that period a woman of the world, and her amatory diversions which served to relieve the tedium of a purely conventional and commercial marriage were tacitly recognized. Intelligent twentieth-century taste is in harmony neither with Victorian sentiments nor with eighteenth-century cicisbeism. It calls for entirely different qualities of sexual attractiveness. Taste changes with cultural circumstances. And with it change the standards of sexual attraction, that is to say, the standards of sexual happiness. Just as the sentiments and tastes of civilized man and woman differ considerably from those which obtain in Central Australia, so the attachment of men and women with minds trained to honest realism must needs differ from that of men and women elaborately trained to pretence, unrealism, and hypocrisy.

The standards of sexual attraction have hitherto been for the most part dictated to women by men. Women have conformed to the pattern demanded by masculine taste and intelligence, to Chinese patterns in China, to Victorian or Georgian patterns in England. To-day, for the first time in historical epochs, women have a say in determining the standards of sexual attraction. There are some women, I am quite aware, who loudly declare that they are entirely unconcerned with sexual attraction. But that lack of intelligence is not worth taking seriously into account. Both women and men are considerably concerned with their own happiness, and if that concern be intelligent and realistic they will be concerned with pleasing one another. The modern intelligent woman is just as much concerned in the matter as was the Chinese patriarchal lady. That is one of the reasons why it would be distasteful to her to adopt commercial prostitution as a profession. In other words her desire to make the most of the opportunities for happiness afforded by sex implies restrictions on promiscuous unchastity. What measure of restriction may be intelligently called for is a matter of cultured realism. If modern intelligence on the part of both men and women can achieve the rounded fufilment of mutual devotion, it will have achieved considerably more than the romantic Victorian ideal commonly succeeded in achieving. If the modern emancipated woman makes it impossible to achieve that fulfilment, she is not so intelligent as she aspires to be.

But whatever the standards of sexual restriction imposed by sexual happiness, they rest upon the consideration of others, of what justice and honesty call for in relations more cultivated and more richly developed than those which suffice in Central Australia. Morality in the relation between the sexes consists ultimately, like morality in every other human relation, in justice and honesty. It does not consist in the length of skirts or in the mystic worth of virginity.

XIV

EMANCIPATED WOMAN AND COERCIVE MORALITY

THE emancipation of women has changed the conditions of marriage. So real is the change that even official theories have had to be adapted to it and modified. Marriage was at first crudely regarded as an economic arrangement; later it was said to be a sacrament. The relation which it established was held to be founded on duty. Greater emphasis is now placed on the view that it is founded on love. It must be admitted that notwithstanding the light thrown on the nature of the institution by the elaborate studies of Adam-and-Eve anthropologists, a good deal of uncertainty still appears to exist as to what marriage is. In all earlier phases of its development the institution of patriarchal marriage was frankly and realistically accepted for what it actually was, a purely economic institution of which the sexual aspect was at most incidental and secondary. The Australian black is, as has been noted, quite clear about the matter. So are the vast majority of people in what we term the lower stages of culture. The majority of people in the higher stages of culture have likewise taken the same view. Marriage was never viewed otherwise than as an economic transaction by the Greeks, and was generally regarded in the same light by the Romans. The economic aspect of marriage was, down to quite recent times, still the most prominent one in Europe. In seventeenth-century England marriage was, a social historian writes, " very much a commercial proceeding, so much portion against so much income." A gentleman of that period wrote: " I mean to marry my daughter to £2,000 a year." The doctrine that marriage is the natural outcome of love developed in Christian times, and very much more slowly than is generally thought. Love-matches were, down to the last century, talked about as exceptional and looked upon as somewhat scandalous. The revolt against patriarchal marriage which is reaching a crisis in our own day began amid the revolutionary democratic movements of the eighteenth and nineteenth centuries, when women like Elizabeth Montague, Fanny Burney, Elizabeth Carter, foreshadowed the modern woman. Those advanced women put forward the libertine notion that marriages which were not love-matches were intolerable abominations. Nineteenth-century democracy has tended to adopt that heresy. It has moreover tended to convert the convention that marriage is the outcome of love into a reality. The advanced women of the nineteenth century revolted against economic marriage. Victorian novels turn upon that advanced view; their usual theme is the triumph of love over the economic and social arrangements hitherto regarded as normal. Love-matches, instead of being the exception, became the rule, and the feeling developed that marriages which are not love-matches are immoral. By an amusing obliteration of historical perspective the simple-minded Adam-and-Eve anthropologists who evoked such applause that they were at once erected into classic authorities, could gravely put forward the story that patriarchal marriage has consisted in love-matches since the days of Adam and Eve, that is to say, of the Australian black.

The view that patriarchal marriage is immoral when it is contracted between persons who do not love each other did not, however, take into consideration that it must become immoral should they cease to love each other. The nineteenth-century novel invariably terminated at marriage. That flagrant lack of logic excites the disgust of the modern intelligent woman. While the advanced woman of the early nineteenth century was so bold as to express the shocking opinion that marriage should be founded on love, the advanced woman of the twentieth century is disposed to discount that opinion as silly sentimental twaddle. Her realism, seasoned with indignant revolt against patriarchal principles and the sentimental subterfuges employed to whitewash them, aims with an intellectual honesty which cannot be too highly admired at reducing the relations between the sexes to brass tacks. She thus reverts to a view of the institution which is nearer to its primitive intention than to the Victorian interpretation, and reasserts the economic as against the sentimental view of it. The ingenious method developed by the nineteenth century into a coarse art, of whitewashing abuses by sentimentalizing them, of whitewashing predatory imperialism, for instance, by reference to the white man's burden and our moral responsibility, or patriarchal economic marriage by Adam-and-Eve anthropology, has caused sentiment to become as a red rag to the infuriated bull of modern intellectual revolt against humbug. That revolt has led to the psychological fact being overlooked that every human relation rests upon sentiment, a fact disguised by the nauseating practice of whitewashing human relations

which rest upon predatory sentiments by representing
them as founded upon noble and tender sentiments.
Sentimentality has done its best to abolish sentiment.

The relation between the sexes is, among the most reflex
and physiological animal organisms, not exclusively physiological, but in the measure of their organization psycho-
physiological. It cannot therefore be completely reduced to
brass tacks of physiology. The possible variations on the
theme of that relation do not consist in a choice between
physiological brass tacks and psychological sentiments, but
between one form of sentiment and another, as between
predatory-individualistic and social-human sentiment. To
cut out social-human sentiments does not bring us down
to the brass tacks of physiology, but to the predatory and
defensive hostile encounter of sex-antagonism.

The very real sentiments which may be associated with
sexual attraction are largely the effect of cultural and social
circumstances—being human and social, they cannot very
well be anything else than cultural. Their form is accordingly determined by social circumstances. The Chinese
had a whole literature, written mostly by women for
women, devoted to the cultivation of exquisite patriarchal-
wifely sentiments. As a result of that literary influence,
Chinese girls used to be convulsed with hysterical flutters
of passionate patriarchal-wifely emotion in reference to the
bridegroom on whom they had never set eyes, and used to
kill themselves in an ecstasy of romantic, dutiful despair
if he happened to die before they had seen him. Those
Chinese literary influences were the counterpart in the
Flowery Land of the novels which our grandmothers fed

on, and which set forth in detailed variety the emotions which a Victorian young lady was expected to feel in regard to the future master whose devoted wife she was destined to become. So great is the power of the pen that, like her Chinese sister, she actually felt the emotions she was expected to feel. A similar literature is even to-day served up to, and consumed by, servant-girls and shop-assistants, and the best specimens of it published, I believe, serially under the title of *Christian Novels*. The effect of that literature upon the modern intelligent woman is, of course, to give her the belly-ache.

When it is stated that the emancipation of women has shifted the foundations of patriarchal marriage, the existence of the shop-girls who read *Christian Novels* is not forgotten, nor that of thousands of women in respectable County families who go to church and read the *Morning Post*. People are still to be found who chip flints. In a progressive country like China the old notion that the wife is the shadow of her husband, which was universally held thirty years ago, has, I am informed, completely disappeared. But in a conservative country like England the majority of respectable County families continue, to the delight of the archæologist, to have their spiritual home in the Middle Ages. The survival of people who are still in the Stone Age or in the Middle Ages ought to be carefully encouraged in the interests of archæological science, but it has little to do with the fact that we are living in the twentieth century and with the general trend of human social evolution. Generations of women have grown up, and some are already getting middle-aged and old-fashioned, who instead of reading *Christian Novels* have read all sorts of books, and even written some, which, had they fallen into the hands of our grandmothers, would have brought on an alarming attack of nerves. To those generations of women the Middle Ages appear to belong to a remote period of history notwithstanding picturesque relics like Salisbury Cathedral, respectable County families, and the *Morning Post*. And so real is the effect of those women on the institution of marriage that the latter has had to be reinterpreted in view of them even by judges most eminent for judicial ignorance.

The question has arisen : " Is it possible to marry those women ? " From the patriarchal point of view it is quite impossible. Hence the fears for the sanctity of the institution, and the lame attempts to derive comfort from the archæological survival of respectable County families. But, on the other hand, it is just as impossible for an intelligent twentieth-century man to marry a lady of a respectable County family. It would be easier and less disastrous for a retired colonel to marry a modern woman. Strangely enough, the emancipation of modern woman and the discarding by her of *Christian Novels* and the *Morning Post,* phenomena which appear to imperil the institution of patriarchal marriage, render the continued and contented association of an intelligent man with a woman for the first time possible.

Broadly speaking, the success of such an association depends on knowing what one is about. The man and the woman who agree to make common cause are likely to cohabit with great success if they thoroughly understand what they are about, and to make a deplorable hash of it if they do not. That is why it was customary for the parson who assisted a man in seducing a woman into patriarchal marriage, or even for the Register clerk who usurped the parson's holy office, to make a little discourse setting forth what patriarchal marriage is not. No precaution was omitted in the Days of Ignorance to ensure that the man and woman about to be " married " by a parson or clerk should not know what they were about. The plan, paradoxical as it may seem, worked well enough in the Days of Ignorance. The woman being thoroughly imbued with the notion that her part was to submit, obey, and suffer in silence, was prepared to do so. The man being equally convinced that he was the sole arbiter, was rather satisfied with a state of things in thorough harmony with his masculine biological instincts. If the woman had red eyes and looked the picture of misery, this was not altogether ungratifying to his biological sadism. He might remind her of her duty, and ask the vicar to have a quiet talk with her on the subject, and she, having had her mind refreshed by the admonitions of religion, would recognize her fault and unreasonableness and would endeavour to be a better Christian in future. The vicar is perfectly right in maintaining that the intelligence of the modern woman and the dissolubility of marriage is fatal to that state of things.

If it is, so much the better. But it is quite another matter to say that it has rendered the association of man and woman impossible. The emancipation of women has, properly speaking, made marriage, for the first time since the origin of the institution, possible. For it has made

N

possible a personal association between man and woman
founded, not upon economic pressure, barbaric claims,
superstitious and coercive sacraments, transient emotional
states or fictitious literary sentimentalities, but upon intelligence. That is the only kind of foundation which has not
hitherto been adduced as an ingenious apologetic justification of the institution. And it has not been mentioned
because women have, under patriarchal Christian institutions, been prevented from developing intelligence. I am not
implying that all modern women are intelligent, any more
than all modern men are intelligent. But they have at least
the same opportunity as modern men to develop intelligence. And therefore a man and a woman are now for the
first time since the savage institution of economic marriage
in a position to enter into the close association of married
cohabitation with a fair knowledge of what they are about,
and with no visionary and hypocritical delusions on the
subject. They are in a position to do so for the sole purpose
of promoting human happiness and with an intelligent
understanding of the conditions which make for that
happiness in the relations between the sexes, and not, as
hitherto, on unjust, inadequate, and fictitious grounds. The
decay of patriarchal marriage should logically result in a
boom in happy marriages.

The moral despots who are concerned for the sanctity of
the institution of marriage are, however, nowise interested
in that issue. They do not care two straws about human
happiness; what they are concerned with is the putting
down of fornication. That happy marriages are twice as
common as under Victorian patriarchal Puritanism is to

them a matter of indifference, if unmarried fornication be also more common. Those who are concerned with the sanctity of marriage are prepared to bear with fortitude the misery of innumerable intolerable marriages so long as there is no promiscuity. It is not for married happiness that they are anxious, but for married indissolubility and sexual coercion. That is the Christian view, the genuine Pauline doctrine. The object of marriage, in the Christian theory, is neither justice nor the successful association of men and women, but the prevention of fornication. That, and not human happiness, is the ground for the sanctity of marriage. It does not derive from social, cultural, human, or reasonable considerations, but from the tabu on fornication. And accordingly the safeguarding of the sanctity of marriage, like the safeguarding of public morals by fig-leaves and the suppression of literature, is not a matter of concern for human happiness, of justice, of reason, or even of sentiment, but a matter of coercion superstitiously, fanatically, and tyrannically imposed.

Whatsoever is desirable in the relation between the sexes, as in all other human relations, is not to be secured or promoted by coercion. The Christian system of morality and the Christian doctrine of marriage are condemned, if for no other reason, because they are systems of coercion. Coercion is becoming impracticable. It was practicable in the Middle Ages when all human relations were founded upon it. Coercive marriage was practicable so long as women accepted patriarchal principles. It is no longer practicable and can never again become so because exploded dogmatic absolutism can never be reinstated. From the

Christian point of view marriage, being a tabu, is not susceptible of discussion. Those who repudiate the authority of tabus cannot be argued with on Christian lines. The redemption of sex relations from the chaos of suffering into which they have been plunged by Christian doctrine depends upon discussion and understanding. That discussion, however unpalatable it may be, however foolish and uninformed much of it is, will continue so long as tabus are imposed by coercion. For the generations now growing up coercion will at least not be secured by the tabu of silence.

The immoral doctrine that morality, or what is held to be morality, is a matter of coercion assumes that the relations between the sexes are susceptible of standardization. The assumption has sunk so deep into Western consciousness that it is for the most part retained by the Puritans who revolt against the immorality of Puritan morals. They are eager to legislate on sex relations and to establish new moral principles. The fact is that the relations between the sexes are of all human relations the last to be amenable to legislation or standardization. Standard laws, juridic or traditional, of sex-morality have never in any age been generally observed. Under whatever system of sexual morality, there will always be abundant immorality. The ineffable Jix delivers himself of the following exquisite asininity : " By the spread of education and the extension of religion in the hearts of the people they will themselves learn to reject all forms of unpleasant conduct, literature, art—and beyond all, of personal thought. If the people learn, not merely to disregard, but to detest all these forms of indecency in thought, word, or deed, the day will come when no form of censorship will be needed, when there will be no prosecutions for breaches of the law."[1] Two thousand years of sexual coercion have brought the vision of fatuous Evangelical pew-openers no nearer to fulfilment. They have brought about quite opposite effects. And no form of sexual restriction, however broad in its scope, has any better chance of success than the pew-opener's dream of despotism. In the lowest savage cultures the only restriction to which sex relations are subject are those represented by the law of exogamy, which corresponds, though it is much wider in scope, to the prohibition of incest. That restrictive law is not only rigorously enforced, but it inspires the savage, in Australia for instance, with the utmost awe. Yet it is constantly broken.

The impossibility of enforcing the observance of any coercive sexual morality is not solely due to the violence of biological urges. It is due to the impossibility of standardizing human outlooks, human nature, and the reactions of human life. It is due to the fact that sexual conduct depends upon those factors, and is therefore no more a proper field for coercion than are human opinions and beliefs. All laws are liable to be broken, else there would be no need for laws. The law against murder is always liable to be broken; it has to be enforced coercively. But the social necessity of securing protection against murder is not a matter of opinion, of human outlook. Laws for the coercive suppression of murder are rightly retained; laws for the coercive suppression of opinions have perforce

[1] Viscount Brentford, *Do We Need a Censor?*, p. 24.

had to be abandoned by despotic powers anxious to enforce them. Coercive sex laws are laws for the enforcement of tabus by coercion. The Christian enterprise of suppressing fornication and banking up the biological urges of men and women within coercive monogamic and indissoluble marriage is the most visionary scheme of religious despotism that has ever been contemplated. There has never been any approach to its successful enforcement, and there is no more rational justification for such enforcement than there ever was for the coercion of opinion.

The Christian scheme is founded upon a superstitious tabu reinforced by barbaric patriarchal claims. But the most reasonable, the wisest, and the most beneficent view of the relations between the sexes has no more claim to be enforced coercively than the Roman Inquisition has a claim to enforce its views by the burning of heretics. So long as they do not give rise to unjust and fraudulent behaviour, views on the relations of the sexes are no more a fit subject for coercive enforcement than views on astronomy or metaphysics. I personally believe that monogamic association is far wiser and beneficent than promiscuity, and that if it can be lifelong and indissoluble, so much the better. But I would sooner that unrestricted promiscuity should be universal than that monogamic association should be universally enforced by coercion.

Coercion was until lately carried out with virtual success in one respect. Women were under the patriarchal system more or less successfully coerced. The coercion of women is no longer possible. That is the revolution which has been brought about by the emancipation of women. It is idle to remark that the emancipation of women is as yet by no means complete, that they are still subject to a good deal of economic and social restriction. They no longer accept patriarchal principles of coercion. It is that repudiation of patriarchal principles by women, and not any vote or economic change, which constitutes their emancipation. And it is that circumstance which also constitutes what some term the sexual revolution. It cannot be rescinded. The sentiment of democratic justice cannot go back on the emancipation of women from coercion. The only form of sexual coercion which has hitherto been successfully applied can no longer be applied in the same manner.

At the conclusion of my work on the anthropology of sex relations, I stated in what some have been so kind as to call " an eloquent peroration," that " the future of the relation between the sexes and of marriage institutions lies with women." [1] Some critics took exception to that " eloquent peroration " on the score that it savoured of sentimental feminism. I had not the remotest intention of being sentimental. I was, on the contrary, being sternly realistic. The passing of the only form of sexual coercion which has been hitherto possible and effectual throws the whole determination of the trend of sex behaviour and marriage upon women. Patriarchal marriage and Christian sex-morality have hitherto been enforced, in a more or less general manner, by coercing women and by taking precautions to prevent them from becoming intelligent. This can no longer be done. There is no other alternative than to persuade them. Parsons, being no longer able to coerce women, can only renew their efforts to seduce them. But

[1] *The Mothers*, Vol. III, p. 516.

principles which claim absolute authority and disclaim discussion are better adapted to coercion than to persuasive seduction. Parsons find intelligent women more difficult to seduce than their patriarchal grandmothers.

The traditional habit of relying upon coercion leads to the assumption that the only alternative to coercive patriarchal marriage is promiscuity. The assumption is not calculated to enhance the reasonableness of coercive morality, and is, of course, in flat contradiction with Adam-and-Eve anthropology. Darwin says that the approximation to monogamy in the sexual life of some animals is due to their lack of intelligence. It appears to be assumed that approximation to intelligence in women emancipated from patriarchal principles implies as a necessary corollary the adoption of promiscuity. If promiscuity is the inevitable outcome of intelligence, no intelligent objection can, of course, be raised against it. If, on the other hand, there are intelligent grounds for objecting to promiscuity, they are more likely to appeal to the intelligent modern woman than to the unintelligent Victorian one. (To become entangled in such elementary logical contradictions is the inevitable drawback to causes which repudiate intelligent and intelligible foundations.) " Promiscuity " is, like most words which represent traditional sexual values, a term of abuse. In point of fact promiscuity is an unattainable ideal. The term of abuse is applied by patriarchal moralists in civilized countries to all sex relations outside coercive patriarchal marriage. A degree of promiscuity a hundred times greater is, in a savage society, described by Adam-and-Eve anthropologists as savage virtue. Both men and women do, always have done, and always will, indulge in varying degrees of

" promiscuity." But to suppose that all women as soon as they repudiate coercion will adopt promiscuity is as fantastic as to suppose that but for the police they will attend the Ascot races stark naked.

Undoubtedly the emancipation of women from coercive patriarchal principles will lead, and has already led—as shown by the slump in prostitution—to an increase in promiscuity. The fact is not to be denied because it is stated in offensive condemnatory terms. The terms are offensive on the Christian premise that fornication is in itself a sin. But the premise has never been proved. What can, in a general way, be proved is that in the present state of culture for the majority of civilized men and women to adopt extensive promiscuity as the only form of sex relation would be injudicious, and unsatisfactory. But it is doubly unsatisfactory when that promiscuity which has always taken place and always will is associated with the profession of monogamic fidelity. It is more than unsatisfactory; it is unjust and disgustingly hypocritical. There was in the eighteenth and early nineteenth century as much promiscuity, probably, as there is at the present day. That promiscuity took the form of infidelity, that is, of fraud and deception. Is it more moral and satisfactory that promiscuity should be fraudulent and clandestine, or open and honest?

Monogamic association is, I said, the most desirable form of association. But the desirability of that intelligent and difficult relation vanishes entirely when it is coercively imposed upon a woman who repudiates it. That is why standardization of sexual behaviour cannot be reasonably secured coercively. Many men and women considerately believe that monogamic association is unsatisfactory. To coerce them into monogamic association or the pretence of it is not only unreasonable and unsatisfactory, but outrageously despotic. The free woman who is freely promiscuous to the extent that she pleases is assuredly in every way more reputable than the promiscuous woman who professes monogamic conventions. It may be doubted whether those conventions materially affect the extent of promiscuity; they mainly affect the extent of vile and nauseating hypocrisy. Does anyone seriously suppose that the woman who is by conviction or by temperament promiscuous will contribute to her own or to anyone else's happiness by becoming a patriarchal wife? That, of course, is what patriarchal Christian morality, being entirely unconcerned with happiness and solely intent on putting down fornication, proposes to do with her. It did it when it could censor her intelligence. Even more commonly it coerced men with lively biological masculine instincts of promiscuity into the sanctified estate of indissoluble patriarchal marriage. Was any formulable human good achieved thereby? Have the results been even favourable to the sanctity of the institution? If the just Nemesis which is overtaking that institution leads to an extension of promiscuity, it only does so by curtailing the excess of suffering and injustice for which the coercive institution has to answer.

That the repudiation by women of coercive sexual control must inevitably imply a return to savage promiscuity is as much a fallacy as the notion entertained by some intelligent women that the abolition of patriarchal principles implies a return to savage matriarchy. Primitive savage matriarchy so-called—which differed considerably from what the term suggests—rested upon social and economic conditions differing entirely from any which are possible in civilized society. The clock can no more be set back to primitive matriarchy than to palæolithic industrial culture. Similarly savage promiscuity rests upon conditions, both social and cultural, to which the social and cultural clock cannot be set back. The cultural psychological products of patriarchal civilization can no more be abolished by the repudiation of patriarchal principles than can its scientific and industrial products by anything short of a cataclysm. Nor is it desirable that they should be. Patriarchal culture has perpetuated an intolerable amount of savage and barbaric superstitions, but it has also created valuable products of cultural civilization. Because the intelligent woman is ready to jettison the savage and barbaric superstitions and outrages of patriarchal civilization, it does not follow that she is equally ready to discard the automobiles and the pretty frocks of patriarchal civilization. The æsthetic, psychological, emotional amenities created by patriarchal culture are as little in danger of being discarded by intelligent women. If the ideal of human happiness embodied in the cultural conception of monogamous association is not altogether a fraudulent delusion, its advantages are as likely to be appreciated by intelligent as by unintelligent women. Should it be a fraudulent delusion there is little occasion to be disturbed by its decay. Emancipated and intelligent woman is at least as competent to draw up the balance of the policies of profusion and prudence, of sexual antagonism and sexual harmony and co-operation, of spendthrift youth against insurance for middle-age. Those considerations are not perhaps amenable to standardization by intelligence. Far less by coercive moral tyranny.

XV

EMANCIPATED MAN AND PATRIARCHAL MARRIAGE

PATRIARCHAL principles were entirely in harmony with the biological sexual dispositions of males. So much so that it naturally appears doubtful to most men whether any modification of those principles can ever be in the same degree satisfactory. That the sanctity of the ideal should be jeopardized is, from that point of view, lamentable.

The sole ground for the modern surrender of patriarchal principles is justice. Such is the temper of modern democratic intelligence that while categorical imperatives are tending to lose their authority, the claims of justice have become very much more authoritative than they were in the ages of faith. Other considerations must yield precedence to those claims. Therefore is it that the demand of women for emancipation from patriarchal principles is unanswerable. Even the ideal arrangement of patriarchal marriage in which the woman was completely adapted by sadistic coercion to masculine primary dispositions must give place to the demands of justice, and so long as Western civilization does not revert to ages of faith there is no going back on that demand.

Masculine sexual dispositions have perforce to become adapted to the new situation created by that demand. The crude sexual urges of savage man have become adapted to conditions of higher culture and have undergone what appears as a transformation in the process; the sentiments of sexual love have become associated with the emotions of sexual lust. The sentiments of civilized man himself have undergone innumerable cultural transformations and adaptations. They will in the same manner become modified in adaptation to the new conditions created by the decay of patriarchal principles.

Those conditions minimize the economic aspect of marriage, not from the sentimental reasons which inspired the romantic Victorian's triumph of love over lucre, but from the natural decay of the importance of the family in relation to consolidated property. The psychological aspect is in practice as in theory the chief aspect of the relation. It is customary to speak of it as love. But the term, as it is used, covers every form of psychological and sexual attraction. It includes the merely biological attraction which, for the Oriental for instance, is co-extensive with the connotation of the term. It includes the romantic and sentimental idealization, in reality closely allied to biological attraction, which was cultivated by nineteenth-century sentimentality. That romantic and sentimental love might be termed patriarchal love, for it assumed patriarchal principles. The ideal of womanhood to which it had reference emphasized the gentleness, the tender and admiring devotion, the helplessness, the submissiveness, and the purity of the patriarchally fashioned female. It assumed a womanly character in harmony with the theory of patriarchal marriage, according to which the woman having been " won," by the sentimental and romantic lover, the relation of complete feminine subservience was automatically ensured. In that view the

part of the male was confined to " wooing " and
" winning " the woman, who demonstrated during that
process her purity by her coyness, and her single-eyed
devotion by her inability to resist the surprised delight she
felt at being the unworthy object of the admiration of so
exalted a being. The sentimental and romantic novels of
the nineteenth century accordingly terminated with the
final event of marriage. They were not in the least concerned with what happened after, unless it were to allude
to the prolific fertility of the happy couple. It was assumed
as a matter of undisputable psychology that the young
woman who could inspire an ideal sentimental and
romantic attachment would make a perfect patriarchal
wife, and that the romantic and sentimental couple would
consequently live happily ever after.

The obsolescence of patriarchal principles considerably
alters those psychological assumptions. The relation, for
one thing, can no longer be assumed to culminate in the
" winning " of the young woman. The sentimental problem
is shifted to the question of keeping her. When marriage
ceases to be regarded as final and indissoluble, love and
" wooing," which were irrelevant in indissoluble Christian
marriage, continue to be factors after the consecration of
the association. It can no longer be assumed that living
happily ever after automatically follows. Love in relation
to marriage is, in short, no longer confined to the problem
of " winning " the woman; the " winning " is imperative
throughout the duration of the association. The difference
is almost as momentous as that between the crude
economic relation of the savage and that of romantic

European tradition. Christian marriage stands in the same relation to the modern conception of successful marriage as the marriage of a Hottentot does to civilized marriage. It is evident that the shifting of the problem from the winning of affection to the keeping of it, may be called a higher conception of the relation, in the same manner as the assumed need of falling in love implies a higher conception than the economic transaction of the savage. Christian marriage was, properly speaking, merely a variety of seduction. Marriage emancipated from Christian sanctity implies honourable intentions, as opposed to the dishonourable intentions of Christian marriage in which, the woman having been seduced, her hopeless condition is irremediable.

Patriarchal marriage did not originally imply sexual fidelity. In the majority of lower cultures so long as the husband's economic possession of the wife is assured, no importance is attached to exclusive sexual possession. The slow development of the claim is not connected with considerations of sentimental personal attachment, but with very crude considerations of proprietary exclusiveness and of juridic legitimacy of the offspring, as heirs to property or position. Often, as in China or in ancient Greece, the claim to the fidelity of the woman in no way implied a corresponding obligation on the part of the man. Until quite recent years, while adultery of the woman constituted in English law a ground for divorce, adultery of the man did not. It is still understood, as it always has been, that sexual infidelity on the part of the man constitutes but a venial offence, while on the part of the woman it constitutes a grave one.

Those crude barbaric motives of savage and Christian culture are entirely supplanted by other sentiments when the man-woman association comes to be transferred to a psychological basis. Mutual sexual fidelity comes to be accounted of the essence of the relation because it is implied in that psychological basis. Infidelity is not a legitimate ground for the dissolution of the relation; it constitutes that dissolution. Professor Westermarck, the protagonist of Adam-and-Eve anthropology, put forward the theory that the institution of marriage owed its origin primarily to the sentiment of masculine jealousy, which, he supposed, required exclusive sexual rights. No notion could be in more glaring contradiction with the facts of ethnology and primitive psychology. What is termed sexual jealousy in animals and in the men of lower cultures is not resentment at sexual infidelity, but sexual frustration. Neither animals nor primitive men resent infidelity, for they know no personal sexual attachment; they resent the loss of a female. And barbaric jealousy has not been the outcome of the growth of personal sexual attachment, but of despotic proprietary claims in privileged classes and chiefs.

The grounds for the sentiment have thus become entirely transformed by cultural and social factors. They have, with the development of personal sexual attachment, become transferred from juridic to emotional values, in the same manner as the association of marriage itself has become similarly transferred from an economic and juridic basis to an emotional one. Sexual fidelity was a juridic claim; it has become an elementary loyalty which is part and parcel of the sentiment that constitutes the only valid and realistic basis of the man-woman association.

The consideration which, in masculine consciousness, weighs perhaps most in favour of patriarchal moral tradition is the value set upon pre-nuptial chastity in women. The entire edifice of sexual restrictive values, the conception of purity, the censorship of sex, in a sense rest ultimately upon that claim. It is one of the strangest facts of cultural history that the claim upon which the authority of sexual moral values so largely depends owes its origin to the most casual and obsolete cultural circumstances. The retrospective claim to bridal virginity developed out of the savage practice of infant-betrothal which modern civilized sentiment utterly repudiates and strives to put down in the more backward societies over which Europeans rule. In the great majority of lower cultural phases bridal virginity is not only not esteemed, but positively resented. A whole series of customs is expressly designed to secure against the marrying of a virgin. Pre-nuptial sexual experience and pre-nuptial motherhood are in most uncultured societies regarded as valuable assets. The development of the claim to bridal virginity is the product of social and economic motives even more crudely sordid than those which have given rise to the claim to married fidelity. It has even less to do with emotional motives and sentiments of personal attachment. And yet no claim of patriarchal moral tradition appears to be more realistic in the validity of its appeal.

The reason is again that the grounds for sexual association have become transferred from the sphere of impersonal social and economic motives to that of personal and emotional relations. It is usual to exclaim that the exaggerated importance ascribed to physical virginity, to the drop of blood of Mosaic tradition, which Orientals are in the habit of securing in their wedding-customs by a judicious provision of pigeon's or rabbit's gore, is the most patent of superstitions. The fact is that it is not the drop of blood, the physical virginity, which is of account, but the emotional virginity which, apart from any patriarchal convention of more or less fictitious " purity," marks the first love in woman with a quality which in most instances cannot be recaptured. That emotional value is of even more account to woman than to man. It cannot be lightly dismissed as wholly irrelevant, whatever allowance be made for the cultural exaggerations of insistent tradition. Nor, of course, can it afford a particle of justification for coercive principles.

The fundamental problems of the personal sex relation, those problems which, in D. H. Lawrence's phrase, constitute the Sphinx's riddle of man's emotional life, which he must answer or be torn to pieces, are not problems of coercion either by social laws or moral principles; they are problems of understanding and adaptation. Patriarchal morality sought to achieve that adaptation unisexually, by the moral and juridic coercion of women in accordance with the direct demands of masculine sexual dispositions. That unisexual adaptation is no longer possible, even were it desirable. Any feminist vision of pseudo-matriarchal unisexual adaptation is even more impracticable and self-defeating. In truth both attitudes are equally opposed to the full realization of the man-woman relation in the social-cultural maturity of its development. The adaptation must be a mutual one. It is natural that the ideals of modern woman, freshly emancipated from the injustice of patriarchal principles, should centre about her independence. But in the subordination of all considerations to that ideal she runs the risk of repeating the most fatal blunder of patriarchal society. In setting up under the disguise of independence the self-defensive individualism of predatory competitive society, she is aping man's most baneful error. Self-defensive individualism is the canker which is eating at the vitals of man-made society, and which bodes its certain doom. To imitate it, to set round life's values the strangle-hold of individualistic self-defensive barriers, is not a manifestation of strength, but of weakness. If any man-woman relation of association is recognized, it is a relation of co-operation, not of strategical self-defence. If that co-operation be a visionary and impossible ideal, there is no alternative but the biological sex-battle, no sexual organization but promiscuity. Social and cultural conditions are not biological, they are artificial, as is all that men and women value. The man-woman relation is not, as Christian patriarchal tradition has so zealously represented, the act of signing away individual existence on the register of a clerk or verger, and leaving the rest to the biological order of the universe. It is a human achievement, a work of art. An achievement in which the principles of self-defensive individualism, of " getting the best of the bargain," of sex-antagonism, are as irrelevant and as fatal as the principles of coercive morality.

The situation created by the emancipation of woman from patriarchal principles is not, as ostrich observers delight in suggesting, a transient mood. But emancipated woman's natural and extreme reaction is. In the heat of that reaction she has good ground to set her independence in the forefront of her interests. She has yet much to win from age-long social tradition in that respect. It is but natural that she should lay the emphasis on her independence. But no form of association can be a relation of independence, any more than any form of stable social structure can be a mere aggregation of individualisms. Association implies, not independence or dependence, but interdependence. Women can, of course, never be independent. Neither can men. If a woman with a settled income of a few hundred thousands kept a harem of male slaves, she would be just as subject to masculine influence as the hen-pecked sultan who kept a harem of female slaves was subjected to feminine influence. Nor could revolted woman compass independence by the manufacture of babies in glass bottles. Reproduction *in vitro*, the dream of feministic independence, would no more abolish sexual interdependence than, except by the production of a race of monsters, it would abolish art and literature. Cultural sex interdependence is not the same thing as biological sex interdependence. Man is dependent upon woman, as woman is dependent upon man, for reasons even deeper than physiological or economic reasons. They are interdependent because self-defensive, strategic, competitive, protective individualistic isolation is intolerable. That is why the crude patriarchal economic and wholly unsentimental institution of marriage of savage society has developed into a relation in which the psychological relation has perforce become primary and the biological and economic relations secondary. To the male of cultured, individualistic society a woman is something more than a sexual prey. She is a surrogate of the mother. She is, despite all the falsifications and stultifications of sugary traditions of sentimentality, the only refuge from self-defensive individualistic independence. He is more abjectly dependent than the most dependent of patriarchal wives. Sexual interdependence implies dependence on the part of both sexes. Their adaptation to that interdependence implies that neither shall abuse the power which is afforded by the dependence of the other. The woman who abuses her sex power is as unjust as the man who abuses his economic power.

The task of mutual adaptation is not an easy one, but upon its achievement depends ultimately human happiness. It is not likely to be promoted by sex-antagonism. Still less can it be aided by coercive morality. Men should frankly renounce every coercive principle of patriarchal tradition. Women should renounce the distorted outlook of sex-antagonism.

XVI

THE FUTURE OF COERCIVE MORALITY

The fierce zeal shown by the conservative elements in Western culture for coercive sex-morality and coercive marriage does not arise from concern for justice or human happiness. It scarcely even professes to do so. That zeal " does not rest on our duty to others." It rests on the tabu upon sex as sinful. That tabu has its root in savage conceptions of magic so primitive and gross that they are no longer generally understood and in the equally exotic doctrine of certain Jewish theosophical sects of two thousand years ago that the object of life is to accumulate treasures in heaven by abnegation. Those savage conceptions and that doctrine are not to any appreciable extent held at the present day. Except from the point of view of the archæological historian, they would not be worth discussing in the twentieth century, but for the circumstance that they constitute the foundation of Western so-called moral tradition, of that coercive sex-morality which is enforced with a zeal exceeding any that is called forth by concern for justice or human welfare. That pseudo-moral tradition is religious; the tyranny which it exercises over Western culture is a religious tyranny. It is the survival in the twentieth century of the tyranny which fought freedom with faggots. The fact should be clearly kept in view. When discussing marriage institutions or sex-morality it is usual to dwell on considerations of social welfare, of psychology, of human happiness. The traditional sex-morality which is under discussion is concerned with none of those things. It " does not rest on our duty to others." It is concerned with the observance of a tabu and with tabu values. It does not take its stand on justice, on social welfare, on the promotion of human happiness. It takes its stand on religion. The atrocious English legislation on marriage is entirely governed by the principles of the Christian religion. In administering it English judges change their gowns for surplices. They are, when carrying out their duties, acting as the " secular arm " of the Church in precisely the same manner as when formerly they burned heretics committed to them by ecclesiastical courts. Official moral censorship, the so-called " safeguarding of public morals," is likewise dictated wholly by the same principles. The officials charged with the safeguarding of public morals are customarily appointed according to their standing as vestrymen and pew-openers. " I am, as is perhaps well known, a Protestant," says the inimitable Jix. Marriage laws, the coercive control of the most personal relations of human life, the so-called moral control of literature and art, the values governing the relations between the sexes and all that has reference to those relations, are in the Western tradition of the present day manifestations of the power claimed by the Churches. That power is but a shadow of what it formerly was. It claimed at one time to control in the like manner the whole political and social life of European nations. It claimed to censor science and thought no less than the sexual morality of literature. Those claims have perforce lapsed. They have been resisted; they have been repelled as an outrageous tyranny.

But that tyranny which has been indignantly shaken off in the spheres of political government, of science, of thought. still reigns supreme in the realm of sex-morality. At the present moment the British government is protesting indignantly against the attempt of a Church to dictate to it its policy in a British dependence. But it sets down in its statutes the coercive laws governing the most vital relations of human life at the dictation of the Church and upon the basis of its superstitious tabus. The Christian Churches formerly claimed to be the dispensers of thought; they now claim to be the dispensers of morals. The one claim is no less outrageous than the other.

The desire of modern men and women to cast off the dead hand of that traditional claim is not a mere revolt of intelligence. Coercive Christian marriage and coercive Christian morality constitute injustices and abuses. They are as such profoundly immoral. Christians are at perfect liberty to believe what they please in morals as in theology. Democratic principles recognize the right of people to be as superstitious as they choose. But they also deny the right of superstitious people to impose their beliefs upon others. Laws which, acting as the secular arm of the Church, enforce Christian tabus and impose Christian marriage coercively are a tyrannous anachronism to be opposed, not in the name of intelligence merely, but in the name of justice and morality. The Pope and the Bishop of London have as much right to place bans on literature, on theatrical plays, and art exhibitions, as I have. Those who place their faith in the judgment of the Pope or of the Bishop of London are at perfect liberty to avoid books, plays, or exhibitions of which they disapprove. But when the police and the Home Secretary take it upon themselves to enforce the Pope's or the Bishop of London's critical judgment, and to act as the secular arms of the Church, they are no longer acting as official servants of a civilized twentieth-century nation, but as familiars of a mediæval inquisition, and they are rendering themselves liable to be treated as all intolerable tyrants are eventually treated.

It is habitually urged by Christians that their sentiments and susceptibilities are entitled to be respected, and that they have the right to claim that they shall not be subjected to offence. Speaking of the police Jixities in Hyde Park, which caused general amusement during his tenure of office, the Home Secretary, Lord Brentford, says: " Hyde Park is paid for by Churchmen, Nonconformists, and Roman Catholics, by decent-minded men and women in all classes of society, and they are not prepared to permit a public park to be degraded in the way in which it undoubtedly and definitely would be if all restrictions on its use were removed." [1] It is hard to apprehend why Churchmen, Nonconformists, and Roman Catholics possess a greater legal right to suppress what " they are not prepared to permit " than atheists. Hyde Park is paid for by atheists as well as by Churchmen, etc. A great many things are permitted and encouraged in Hyde Park which are more deeply offensive and irritating to the feelings and susceptibilities of atheists than the sight of a couple kissing is offensive to Churchmen. Have atheists the right to

[1] Viscount Brentford, *Do We Need a Censor?*, p. 7.

demand that mournful psalm-singing, nigger missionaries, and Salvationist meetings shall be put a stop to in Hyde Park because they are excruciating to their feelings? They have just as much, or as little, as people whose feelings and susceptibilities are irritated by the sight of a couple kissing have the right to use the Home Office and the police to protect their supposed or pretended suscepti- bilities by coercing everyone to conform with them. (If the question of numerical majorities be advanced, the general chorus of derision, ridicule, and protest which greeted the Churchmen's, etc., activities through the secular arm of Vestryman Jix, and compelled him to adopt an apologetic attitude, does not appear to support the claim.) All censorship of so-called public morals, whether in literature, in the theatre, or elsewhere, is the tyrannous imposition by coercion of religious values upon the secular community. Those who claim as a civic right the power to suppress kissing, lately claimed the right to enforce Sabbath-observance and church-going. Those who claim the right to censor the morals of literature, lately claimed the right to censor its theology and its science. Censorship is a tyrannical abuse, no matter where exercised; one form of censorship is no more consistent with just rights than is another. It is not the scope, but the principle of censor- ship which is an outrage. And the principle of coercive censorship is the principle which governs the whole application of Christian doctrines concerning the vileness of sex to the social existence of men and women in Western culture.

The revolt against that coercion is not a licentious, but

a moral revolt. The charge of licentiousness has invariably been brought by theocratic despotism against any attempt to oppose its dictatorship. When in the eighteenth century writers protested against theocratic censorship and *lettres de cachet,* their resistance to absolutism and tyranny was termed licentiousness, and the writers were called " libertines." The licence which modern intelligence claims is that absolutist tabus shall not be accounted substitutes for reason and justice in the most fundamental of human relations. If such licence be contrary to reason and justice, it can be repulsed on grounds of reason and justice. To oppose it on grounds of tabu values, of dogmatic categorical affirmations which repudiate discussion, which cannot be argued, which disclaim duty to others, is an abuse which the moral sense of modern democratic intelligence resists, and will continue to resist until the tyrannical abuse has joined other tyrannical abuses of the past in the Chamber of Horrors of history.

That coercive sexual morality and coercive Christian marriage have produced desirable effects on the relations between the sexes or on the emotional aspects of Western culture is not true. The reverse is the truth. Coercive Christian marriage has produced a mountain-mass of wanton suffering and injustice. Coercive Christian sex values have poisoned the sexual life of Western society. Those manifestations of theocratic tyranny are not to be resisted only because all tyranny should be resisted, but because the substitution of tabus for reason and justice in the relations between the sexes can have none but pernicious effects. The progress of reason and justice in the sphere where hitherto tabus only have ruled has already produced desirable and beneficial results. The revolt of intelligent women against the injustice of coercive patriarchal marriage has not, as is commonly represented, sapped marriage, it has sapped the iniquity of unjust marriage and the misery of coercive marriage. It will continue to do so. It will inevitably abolish eventually the monstrous hypocritical enormity of English marriage legislation. It may quite possibly redeem the association of men and women in durable marriage from the parlous condition of disrepute and decay to which it has been reduced by patriarchal principles and the Christian religion.

Christians will continue to uphold the sanctity of coercive and brutally unjust marriage. None is ever likely to prevent them from doing so. But intelligent men and women are likely to prevent theocratic tyranny from imposing upon them through the secular arm savage tabus and barbaric abuses. Church and State must in this, as in all other spheres, be clearly separated. Marriage, being a private, not a public concern, the State has no right therein except in so far as it may deem it desirable to register the conclusion or the dissolution of the association. Still less has it the right to act in the matter as the secular arm of religious bodies.

The religious sects claim that Western culture is Christian. Unfortunately it is. The ideas, the concepts, the judgments, the languages, the adjectives, the instincts, the very physiological functions of people born in the midst of Western culture are permeated and water-logged with exudations of Christianity. That age-long saturation has given rise to a sodden condition of the cerebral tissues which renders it difficult for them to secrete any but Christian values. So that post-Puritan men and intelligent women who are not Christian are obsessed with the need of sublimating sex relations, which they regard as naturally vile, into pure, beautiful, and noble values. They have forgotten that justice and reason are the first human social values. And when they seek to apply justice and reason to the human relations of Western civilized society, they find that those relations are so hopelessly entangled in Christian values, that reason and justice cannot be applied to them without reconstructing Western civilized society. The rationalization of the relations between the sexes is not possible in a fundamental manner so long as that structure lasts—which will probably not be very long. Tabu coercive marriage cannot be converted into a humanly rational and just institution before Western civilization itself emerges from barbarism. Rational sexual association involves among other things the assured economic independence of women and the assured upbringing of children. The economic independence of women is not possible by their adopting competitive individualism, and it is incompatible with housekeeping. There is no way of securing it except by socialism. (The application of the principles of socialism to women is, by the way, independent of whether or no those principles are applied to men.) The adequate upbringing of children, which in the present stage of culture is entirely impossible by private enterprise and has long ceased, except in cases of the grossest and most scandalous neglect, to be a function of parents, also demands socialism. But those social provisions are quite impracticable while three-fourths of the wealth at the disposal of Western civilization goes up the chimney in the form of payments and preparations for wars. Thus—so ravelled is the entanglement of existing social relations—the rationalization of marriage requires among other things the United States of Europe.

But the changes in the whole attitude of intelligent men and women towards their relations do not depend upon any revolution which may be expected in the future, but on a revolution which has already taken place and is an accomplished fact which nothing can now alter. The categorical authority of coercive patriarchal marriage and coercive Christian morality has passed away so far as intelligent men and women are concerned. The effects of that revolution cannot be obliterated by any ostrich policy; they are independent of any pleas or opinions urged for or against. The question which confronts intelligent men and women is not that which confronted the lady who expressed her willingness to accept the universe. It is not a question of accepting or rejecting existing facts, but of becoming adapted to those facts.

Christian coercive morality is founded upon the value assigned to all that has reference to sex as sin. That value has had two opposite effects: a repressive and inhibitory effect which has given rise to numerous indirect, subtle, disguised, and unrecognized morbid manifestations; an artificial stimulatory effect which has given rise to equally morbid aberrant manifestations which constitute that vileness which distinguishes the sophisticated vice of civilization from the sexuality of natural man. There will probably always be a wide diversity in sexual values, that is to say, a wide diversity in outlooks on sex. The path of adaptation does not consist in efforts to invest sex with new values, to sublimate it, to purify what a morbid cultural tradition has taught to regard as impure. It lies in a clearer appreciation of other values which have been obscured by that tradition. If modern intelligence has revolted against that tradition it is because men and women have been influenced by the moral value of justice and reason. The claim of women to emancipation from patriarchal principles has commanded recognition because it is just and reasonable. Christian moral tradition placed sexual purity at the head of all the virtues and identified sin with sex. It has given rise to the grotesque connotation of Western culture which identifies morality with sexual prohibitions, and consequently relegates justice and intellectual honesty to a lower sphere, not included in the current use of the term morality. The baneful effects of the tabu values of Christian coercive morality, which are opposed in the name of human social values, in the name of justice and honesty, are not to be remedied by endeavouring to invest sex with new artificial values, but by apprehending the fact that the relations between the sexes are, like all other human relations, and in an even higher degree, subject to human social sentiments, to justice, to goodwill, to intellectual honesty. These, and not superstitious ritual purities derived from savage magic, or sin which is the Hebrew equivalent of tabu are the foundations of morality.

If human society, which is an association of men and women, is governed by those social values and not by the tabus of a coercive system of pseudo-morality, sexual values will to a large extent take care of themselves. The obsolescence of coercive tabu-morality does not imply that the biological urges of sex shall be uncontrolled, any more than the obsolescence of the predatory and strategical structure of existing society implies anarchy. Any change from existing conditions is readily denounced as anarchy. The abolition of feudalism was denounced as anarchy, as the abolition of patriarchal principles by the emancipation of women is denounced as sexual anarchy. Association is incompatible with anarchy. So long as men and women regard their relation as an association, and not as a coercive institution, or as a contest of conflicting interests, there can be no anarchy. Human society was originally founded upon a very close association and co-operation between the sexes. It has undergone many changes, and the human mind has undergone much cultural development. The outlook of intelligent men and women differs vastly from that of primitive savages. But inasmuch as human society still consists in an association of men and women, one of the first requirements of its vital structure is still, though on a vastly different plane, harmonious co-operation between the two sexes and mutual justice, goodwill, and loyalty. The demands made on the adaptive control of biological sexual urges by the requirements of that association and interdependence constitute sexual morality. That and nothing else. Men who are influenced by the sense of justice exercise control over their biological urges because they are unwilling to inflict injury upon women. Women who are influenced by like considerations exercise control over their biological urges because they are reluctant to inflict suffering on men.

The extent of that control must necessarily vary greatly in individual men and women. It has always greatly varied, under whatever moral or religious regimen. To hear some Christian moralists one might suppose that under the Christian system of coercive morality, the biological urges of men and women had been completely controlled, that there had been no promiscuity, no adultery, no sexual licence; and that these things, absent under coercive Christian morality, must at once make their appearance for the first time on the removal of that coercion. Everybody knows that the suggestion is grotesquely untrue. Every form of sexual excess, anarchy, and vice has flourished under Christian morality as luxuriously as under pagan morality. All goes to show that there was considerably more promiscuity at the height of Victorian Puritanism than there is anywhere at the present day. The chief difference between Victorian licentiousness and contemporary " immorality " is that the one consisted of clandestine conduct, the other consists of overt principles. The capitulation of the powerful aristocratic classes to bourgeois sanctimony has never been but a hypocritical outward conformity, an abstention from scandal, not from sexual licence. " The code was rigid. Within the closed circle of their own set, anybody

P

might do as they pleased, but no scandal must leak out
to the uninitiated. Appearances must be respected, though
morals might be neglected." [1] English divorce laws have
been fiercely maintained in their barbaric state not from
any regard for the sanctity of marriage, but from the
rigid rule that appearances must be preserved.

And that vile and nauseous code of dissolute ruling
classes is identical with that which is upheld by coercive
Christian moralists. It is the overt profession of opinion,
not the licence of conduct which excites their indignation.
If the choice could be offered between the clandestine
promiscuity associated with rigorous moralistic professions,
and happy, orderly sexual organization attended with open
repudiation of traditional moral tabus, there is not one
who would not choose the hypocritical code. That is also
the reason why the attitude of modern men and women
towards sex is beyond all comparison more self-respecting
than that of the Victorians. Victorian coercive morality
remained self-satisfied so long as sexual licence was conscientiously secretive. English bishops had no objection to
deriving part of their incomes from brothels so long as
they could pretend that they knew nothing about it.
Aristocratic English husbands might keep a seraglio of
mistresses provided that the divorce laws ensured against
the scandal of publicity. Pre-nuptial chastity might be
more or less fictitious, but Christian morality was satisfied
so long as the fiction was not exposed. A wife might dis-
creetly entertain a half-dozen lovers, but Victorian morality
reserved its indignation and its persecuting zeal for the

[1] V. Sackville-West, *The Edwardians*, p. 100.

man and woman who dared to live in model devotion and fidelity while they declined to ask the sanction of the Church for their exemplary union. The head of the offence of modernism in sexual morality is not increased licentiousness, but the repudiation of clandestine, furtive, and secretive licentiousness. Coercive morality never imposed purity, it only exacted hypocrisy.

Sex is no more impure and base than it is noble. But furtiveness, secretiveness, and hypocrisy are base. They have imparted their baseness to biological realities; they have thrust the vileness of secretive hypocrisy upon them. Christian morality has created sin. It has set up the artificial stimulus of tabus to be furtively, secretly, and libidinously broken, and rendered the ingenuity of civilized pruriency morbid as compared with the frank lusts of the savage.

The decay of coercive Christian sexual morality can have none but beneficial results. The sanitary effect of the obsolescence of that furtive and clandestine morality upon the outlook of modern men and women is already inestimable. The resources of obscenity and morbid sexuality are already becoming greatly reduced. There are epicures who are in favour of the rehabilitation of Victorian prudery and Christian purity on account of the enhanced sexual stimulation which they afforded. The banned literature which the modern young woman openly reads is immeasurably healthier than the French novels of the eighties over which her grandmother surreptitiously pored.

No rules or principles or moral doctrines will under any conditions secure the complete adaptation of biological urges to complex social relations. There is no Utopia of universal happiness possible in regard to those relations any more than in regard to economic relations. The only approach to such a Utopia of happiness is that which man and woman can build by individual effort and understanding. Sex, which can be the foundation of that happiness, will continue to be the cause of great suffering also. Coercive morality, coercive marriage have magnified that suffering enormously. Human intelligence has the right to demand, not happiness at all cost, but the abolition of needless and unreasonable suffering.

When, two or three centuries ago, reason revolted against the dogmatism of Christianity, it was denounced as error and licence, and opposed in the name of truth. Christian dogmatism is now compelled to apologize for that intellectual coercion. Present generations are in revolt against the coercive morality of Christianity. The claims of justice and reason are, as of old, branded as licence and opposed in the name of morality. But what is now defended as unquestionable moral authority will one day be seen to be immoral, to be a coercive despotism as indefensible on moral grounds as the opposition of dogmatism to scientific inquiry was indefensible on the ground of truth on which it formerly claimed to stand.

The improvement which is to be looked for from the introduction of justice and reason in the relation between the sexes is not the abolition of moral control over primal biological urges, but the substitution of the control of intelligence and human justice for that of ignorance, fanaticism, and superstition.

PARENTHOOD
A MANUAL OF BIRTH CONTROL
MICHAEL FIELDING
With a Preface by
H. G. WELLS

Revised and greatly extended edition, with diagrams, full bibliography, information as to clinics, etc.

"When the adult citizen has gone through these pages he or she will have all the mastery of his or her sexual self that knowledge can give." *From H. G. Wells' Preface.*

" More likely to be of practical value to the average married couple than anything I have seen."
Norman Haire in The Saturday Review.

"One of the most impartial and balanced discussions of the practical and technical aspects of birth control that has yet appeared " *The Lancet.*

" The handling of this delicate subject is beyond reproach."
The Medical Times.

Paper, 2s.   *Cloth, 3s. 6d.*   *Postage, 2d.*

THE SEX FACTOR
IN MARRIAGE
HELENA WRIGHT, M.B., B.S
With an Introduction by
The Rev. H. GRAY, D.D.

" Dr. Wright has set out simply, decently and without circumlocution, what she believes to be the indispensable minimum of information that all married persons should have about the physiology and anatomy of reproduction and the technique of sexual union." *The Spectator.*

"Twenty years ago there were no books on the physical and physiological side of marriage which were the least use to the young. Since then several have been written, but none so shortly, sensibly and in such good taste as Dr. Wright's. . . . It was badly needed and here it is." *The Nation.*

3s. 6d.

NOEL DOUGLAS, 38 GREAT ORMOND STREET, W.C.1

The Conquest of Happiness

By BERTRAND RUSSELL, F.R.S.

La. Cr. 8vo. Second Impression. 7s. 6d.

" Beautifully planned and written. . . . The author knows just what he wants to say and says it brilliantly. . . . A definitely helpful book, and one that should be kept and consulted in those dark hours that beset us all."—*Spectator.*

" It goes without saying that this book is good reading; indeed, as literature, Mr. Russell has written nothing better. Moreover . . . it is full of wisdom, at once grave and sunny."—*Manchester Guardian.*

Marriage and Morals

By BERTRAND RUSSELL, F.R.S.

La. Cr. 8vo. Fourth Impression. 7s. 6d.

" It is sure to be widely read, since the author is known as one of the finest intellects of our day and as master of a beautiful English style. The book is a derisive and provocative attack on all that a Christian means by morality. . . ."—DEAN INGE in the *Evening Standard.*

" Whatever we may think of his proposals, it is evident that such a book, written by a man whose good faith is above question, is long overdue."—*Spectator.*

The Family

By DR. F. MÜLLER-LYER

Translated by F. W. STELLA BROWNE

Demy 8vo. About 16s.

What were marriage and the family in the " dim red dawn of man "? How have they changed and evolved? What is their probable future? This clear and comprehensive book, written by a leading sociologist, answers these questions with a wealth of material, from a thoroughly modern point of view, and without traditional prejudices.

Birth Control on Trial

By LELLA SECOR FLORENCE

Foreword by

SIR HUMPHRY ROLLESTON, BART., K.C.B., M.D., F.R.C.P.

Cr. 8vo. 5s.

" An extremely valuable volume. . . . Should be read by all interested in this subject."—*British Medical Journal.*
" It will prove of great value. . . . The author writes with impartiality and restraint unusual amongst advocates of birth control."—*Lancet.*
" An admirable piece of research."—*Nation.*

The Modern Attitude to the Sex Problem

By KENNETH INGRAM

Cr. 8vo. 5s.

" A book worth reading, especially by readers to whom the subject of sex psychology is a new and unexplored one."—*The Times.*
" Mr. Kenneth Ingram has been earning for himself a reputation for clear and shrewd thinking. . . . He surpasses himself in this book, which must rank not only as his best but his most useful work."—*Sunday Referee.*

Social Control of Sex Expression

By GEOFFREY MAY, LL.D.
Of the Inner Temple

Demy 8vo. 12s. 6d.

This is a study of the efforts of the State to control the sexual life of the individual. After tracing the formulation of the Christian doctrine of sex repression and its introduction into England, it describes the methods used by the Church to enforce its doctrine, their increasing failure, and the gradual rise to temporal control in the form of Puritanism. It shows how Puritanism, meeting a sudden end in England, continued to dominate sexual expression in America until in both countries new forms of social control rendered the laws obsolescent.

For Product Safety Concerns and Information please contact our EU
representative GPSR@taylorandfrancis.com
Taylor & Francis Verlag GmbH, Kaufingerstraße 24, 80331 München, Germany

www.ingramcontent.com/pod-product-compliance
Lightning Source LLC
Chambersburg PA
CBHW070406270326
41926CB00014B/2722